LOGBOOK OF THE FARALLONES

Logbook
of the
Farallones

BY

MICHAEL WHITT

ILLUSTRATIONS BY
FREDERICK J. WATSON

LA VENTANA PRESS
1998

BOB JONES

The author collecting otoliths on Maintop with Dr. David G. Ainley, kneeling.

BURR HENEMAN

Dr. Ainley weighing storm petrel chicks on Lighthouse Hill

FOR DR. DAVID G. AINLEY

Contents

ISBN 0-9665110-0-X

Published by:
La Ventana Press
P.O. Box 434
Inverness, California 94937

Other books by the author

LA VENTANA
SAWS
COHO
WILD HARVEST

Versions of Chapters I, II, III, IV and VIII
appeared in *Estero*, A West Marin Quarterly

Acknowledgments

This book came very slowly to its present state.

My greatest debt of gratitude is owed Derick Watson, the distinguished British wildlife artist, for providing the fine illustrations for this book. His support was indispensable.

Don Greame Kelley was editing the manuscript at the time of his death. To him I owed special thanks for encouraging me to go ahead with the book. Dr. David Ainley took time out from his busy schedule, which included going over the proofs of a book that covers 16 years of avian research on the Farallones, to read the manuscript and make suggestions and technical corrections. I am grateful to him for this and for having made it possible for me to participate in Point Reyes Bird Observatory's (PRBO) Farallon program. My son Garrett, a graduate of the Journalism School at University of Southern California, also made helpful editorial comments.

I want to thank Jim Lewis for his hospitality on the islands; he always made me feel welcome. He was also the best cook during my time out there. I am grateful to Steve Morrell for making sure that I did not miss the fledging of the murres, an experience that, more than any other, made me determined to finish this book, and for loaning me his photo library on the Farallones for as long as I needed it. I am also grateful to Dr. Malcolm Coulter for introducing me to the weeds and wildflowers of Southeast Farallon. Harriet Huber and Ron LeValley were also helpful.

I want to acknowledge the U.S. Fish and Wildlife Service, whose creative partnership with PRBO has made the Farallon Wildlife Refuge not only a successful sanctuary for wildlife, but a research site of distinction. I am indebted to the United States Coast Guard and to the Farallon Patrol of the Oceanic Society for transportation to and from the Farallones after I sold my boat, and to the U.S. Coast Guard for coming to my aid when *Angelina* was dead in the water and drifting into the surf on Point Reyes Beach. To the crab boat that called the Coast Guard and held me in check until they got there, I will always be in debt. I appreciate the presence of Point Reyes National Seashore, which has protected the Point Reyes Peninsula from development.

Bob Jones of University of California Museum of Vertebrate Zoology and Burr Heneman, former Executive Director of PRBO, were kind enough to loan me photographs. I am also grateful to Dewey Livingston, historian for Point Reyes National Seashore, for his help in locating a picture of Alioto Fish Dock, which has been torn down.

I also want to thank Ed Letter and the board of the Bolinas Rod and Boat Club for letting me use their dock. I am grateful to the people at Boicelli and Mercury Marine Supply at Fisherman's Wharf for their patience in helping me solve the problems that inevitably arise with an old boat, and for letting me tie up once to their dock. Gerald Anderson of the U.S. Coast Guard kept an eye on *Angelina* while she was anchored at Drake Bay and helped keep her in running order. George Nunes of "A" Ranch on the Point Reyes Peninsula was kind enough to loan me his mooring in Drake Bay. He and his wife Betty were also helpful in finding pictures of the old Alioto Fish Dock. Roger Dewey provided me with information on Lloyd Williams. The late Bud Roth of Inverness was generous in assisting with repairs on my boat *Angelina*. I appreciate Clayton Lewis's concern for my well-being offshore and the help he gave me in procuring a direction finder. He also introduced me to the people at Boicelli and Mercury. Eddie Richardson of Inverness, whose boat *Ranger* was anchored near mine, gave me my first and only copy of Chapman's *Piloting, Seamanship and Small Boat Handling*. Carlo Crivello of San Francisco took me salmon fishing on his Monterey and showed me the ropes. Horace Glasson of Bolinas helped me obtain photographs of the mouth of Bolinas lagoon. The late Lyla and Lloyd Williams allowed me access to the Alioto Fish Dock and extended their hospitality to me; Lloyd cleaned and filleted all my fish, even after he showed me how.

I am also grateful to the staff at PRBO, Tom Moritz and Brian Lym of the California Academy of Sciences Library, Bill Kooiman of the Maritime Museum Library, and Tupper Blake for help in research. Pete White, a PRBO volunteer, was a big help in unravelling the mystery of "Billy Pugh."

Susan Acker of Feathered Serpent Press was most generous of her time and varied skills in helping design the logo. Ian Gaffney made the maps.

I want to thank typists Barbara Gunn, Okanta Leonard and Pam Robert – some of whom may have forgotten they typed parts of the manuscript – for perserverance in reading a doctor's handwriting.

Elizabeth Morales designed the book and her decisive approach brought order out of chaos. Elisabeth Ptak gleaned the manuscript of mistakes, and if she missed any, it was only because there were too many for any one mortal to find.

Mike Sykes and Gay Schecter kindly serialized parts of this book in their quarterly *Estero*.

I apologize for any omissions here.

The avian research program on the Farallones, as designed by Dr. Ainley, was conducted in the best scientific traditions, and the opinions, speculations and queries expressed here are mine and are not derived from or implied in that research. Any confusion in the book is strictly a product of my unscholarly meditations.

The Author
Inverness Park, CA
2-18-98

Foreword

This book was written from a detailed journal of my cruises in the Gulf of the Farallones (1971 to 1972) and several later visits to Southeast Farallon. A boat, seabirds, marine mammals, rocks and the sea are the main characters in this story. A few human instances are also included.

The boat in my story is a Monterey fishing boat, *Angelina*, a descendant of the "dago" fishing boat, or as it was officially known, the San Francisco felucca, which was originally lateen-rigged and outfitted with oars. The boats were eventually decked over and a cabin and motor added. They are beautiful and seaworthy craft.

The seabirds and mammals,including humans, are those that breed, nest, visit, rest, roost, haul out, feed and study on the Farallon Islands, or frequent the Gulf of the Farallones, which takes in the waters of the continental shelf from Pillar Point on the south to Point Reyes on the north.

Since my time on the islands when elephant seals were just becoming re-established, the great white shark population has greatly increased along with the numbers of its prey species, the elephant seal. In fact, there is now a considerable amount of research interest in the great white shark at the Farallones. And while I only saw a few gray whales pass by when I was on the islands, many species now frequent the Gulf of the Farallones. The ban on whaling has brought back blue whales, humpback whales, sperm whales, minke whales, killer whales and others to our waters.

The late 1960s and early 1970s marked the beginning of a new era in our awareness of the environment and its degradation. At about the same time, and perhaps as a result of this environmental awakening, the United States Fish and Wildlife Service developed a renewed interest in its jewel, the Farallon National Wildlife Refuge. During this period, the Gulf of the Farallones National Marine Sanctuary was conceived. These were heady times, even for agencies.

F.J.Watson

Introduction

1.

BRIEF HISTORY OF THE FARALLONES

The Miwok Indians living in the vicinity of the great bay later called by the name of San Francisco in honor of St. Francis of Assisi gazed out over the "Sundown Sea" on clear days and imagined the rocks rising near the western horizon to be inhabited by their dead.

These same rocks were first seen by white men in 1543, when the Spanish navigator Ferello of Cabrillo's voyage of discovery named them *Los Farallones*. Farallon is Spanish for cliff or small, rocky island. The Farallon Islands consist of three parts: South Farallones, Middle Farallon and North Farallones. The South Farallones are two islands, Southeast Farallon and West End, divided by a narrow channel; Middle Farallon is a solitary rock three miles north of South Farallones; and the North Farallones, four miles north of Middle Farallon, are a collection of large rocks. Southeast Farallon is the only island in the group inhabited by humans.

In 1775, the name of the islands was enlarged to *Los Farallones de los Frayles*, which means little islands of the friars. The name was meant to honor the monks who participated in the discovery and exploration of San Francisco Bay. It is also poetically descriptive of the islands themselves, for they are set apart from the mainland, appear austere in their gray habit, and provide a sanctuary for "God's" creatures, in this case, seabirds and marine animals.

Francis Drake, the British freebooter, landed on the islands, which he called St. James, in 1579 to provision his ship with seals and birds, thus beginning a practice that resulted in the eventual loss of some species and the radical reduction of others – a trend that was only fully reversed by the partnership of the U.S. Fish and Wildlife Service and Point Reyes Bird Observatory on Southeast Farallon.

In the early 19th century, ships from Boston harvested a "vast number of fur and hair seal" at the Farallones. They were followed by the Russians and their Aleut hunters, who stripped the islands of seals and otters. The Russians maintained a hunting establishment at the Farallones from 1812 to 1840.

Beginning with the Gold Rush, the islands were raided for murre eggs until the murres became almost extinct. The eggers fought and killed each other over this resource. As the wild turkey provided food for the pilgrims, the murres helped feed the first great wave of human migrants to the West Coast – and yet the murre has never been commemorated by California or the federal government.

The first lighthouse was established in 1855, and Southeast Farallon has been continuously inhabited since. The lighthouse keepers' domestic animals (dogs, cats, goats, donkeys and rabbits) destroyed habitat and preyed on wildlife.

Pollution has been a problem since motors replaced sail in commercial shipping. Ships, until recently, customarily pumped their bilges of oily water near the Farallones before entering San Francisco Bay. Several major oil spills in the vicinity have contributed further to the loss of birds and marine mammals.

Nuclear wastes have also been dumped at sea near the islands and repose in drums on the bottom, waiting to explode silently into the food web.

A more recent threat was gill netting. An estimated 25-30,000 murres were killed in 1983 alone. Legislation, mainly under the scientifically-based advocacy of PRBO, has been enacted to control this needless slaughter.

The first step in the reversal of this trend was taken in 1911, when the North Farallones were made a Federal Reserve. In 1968, Point Reyes Bird Observatory began its occupation of Southeast Farallon. In 1969, the Islands' status was upgraded to that of a National Wildlife Refuge, which included Southeast Farallon. In 1974, the light was automated and the Coast Guard departed. For the first time in 400 years the islands, now exclusively in the care of the U.S. Fish and Wildlife Service and PRBO, were free from the threat of exploitation.

2.

POINT REYES BIRD OBSERVATORY

The puzzle of bird migration led to the formation of the first bird observatories. When man began to grow curious about nature and seek a rational explanation for what he observed, he began formulating theories to explain the seasonal appearance and disappearance of birds from his surroundings. Since many birds migrate at night and, in any event, most often depart without notice, their comings and goings were a mystery.

One of the earliest theories concerned swallows, conspicuous in their migratory habits by their large numbers, their occupation of the open sky, where they are easily observed, and the synchrony of their arrival and departure. One theory postulated that swallows descended via the stems of reeds into the mud where they spent the winter. In 1765, the English anatomist and surgeon John Hunter disproved this theory by dissecting a swallow and failing to find any means by which life underwater could be sustained. Still, accounts of digging the hibernating birds out of the mud appeared in the scientific literature as late as the last century.

When it was discovered that birds did migrate, one theory had the smaller and supposedly weaker birds riding on the backs of cranes. Another theory suggested that birds flew high into the sky until they were borne away on winds that "blew between the worlds," perhaps an early intimation of the jet stream.

Though birds have always exercised a strong attraction on the imagination of man, even symbolizing that function of the human brain, they long eluded systematic study by virtue of their stealth and the difficulty of their capture. The distribution of birds is both longitudinal and latitudinal while bird migration is mainly latitudinal; voyages of discovery were generally longitudinal, i.e., along east-west lines, so birds encountered were almost always new species. Even when the voyages were latitudinal, mariners had no reason to suspect that the birds seen at one time of year in one latitude were not different populations from similar species seen elsewhere. Birds were of little interest to early explorers anyway except as food and, later, if a medical doctor, doubling as an ornithologist, were along to collect and prepare the skins, as curiosities to fill bird cases in museums. Their skins were merely some of the exotic trappings of empire. Birds shared the fate of all the lower animals that were appetizing to any degree: they were eaten long before they were understood.

From the beginning, bird observatories were the personal enterprise of curious citizens as well as of scientists. Heinrich Gatke established the first bird observatory (*vogelwarte* in German, which translates to bird lookout) at the turn of the century on Helgoland Island, Germany, in the North Sea. Planning to stay only a short time, he remained on the island for 50 years studying birdlife and migration! A trap, since known as the Helgoland trap, for capturing birds was devised on this island. For the first time, migrants could be reliably caught without harm, examined in the hand and banded or, in European parlance, ringed.

Lord William Percy banded woodcock in Northumberland in the 1880s, and Christian Mortensen, a Dane studying migration, banded starlings in 1899.

Between 1880 and 1888, a migration committee was formed in Britain to collect and correlate data on bird migration from lighthouses and lightships. The first English observatory was not founded until 1927, when R.M. Lockley moved to the uninhabited island of Skokholm off the west coast of England in the Irish Sea. Supporting himself by fishing and sheep raising, he became a devoted student of seabirds. In 1933, he built a trap modeled on the Helgoland prototype for capturing and banding migrants. The publication of his papers brought a large number of bird enthusiasts to the island and began a tradition of visitation that still exists today at English observatories.

The success of the trapping and banding program on Skokholm led to the establishment of other bird observatories. Even World War II could not completely halt their proliferation, one being conceived by a British soldier while he was a prisoner-of-war.

The banding program was given a great boost by the advent of the mist net, which enabled banding activities to be easily conducted on a portable basis.

A Bird Observatories Committee was formed in Britain in 1946 to define the purpose and co-ordinate the activities of British bird observatories. This definition of a bird observatory was provided by the Committee: "A field station co-operatively manned for the purpose of making continuous observations on migrant birds and for catching, examining and marking them." Today there are more than a dozen official bird observatories operating in Britian.

In 1916, the U.S. and Canada signed the Convention for the Protection of Migratory Birds, which was designed to guarantee the welfare of migrants on both sides of the border. (Unfortunately, Latin America was not a party to the Convention, and provision for the protection of the birds' habitat was omitted.) The U.S. Fish and Wildlife Service was made responsible for the welfare of migrants and for the administration of our banding program.

Point Reyes Bird Observatory, an independent organization based on the British model, was founded in 1965 through the combined efforts of Dr. Richard Mewaldt of San Jose State University, local members of the Western Bird Banding Association, including Rich Stallcup, and Point Reyes National Seashore. The seed for America's first bird observatory had been planted in the minds of members of the Western Bird Banding Association by Guy McCaskie, a Scots birder. The original headquarters were located at the old Heims Ranch in Point Reyes National Seashore, hence the name Point Reyes Bird Observatory. Point Reyes was chosen for the many species of birds recorded there, including a large number of rare migrants; it is also public land. The original purpose of Point Reyes Bird Observatory, the first bird station of its kind in the U.S., was the same as that of its British forbears. It subsequently moved to Palomarin outside Bolinas (its location during the time of the events in this book). Palomarin remains as a landbird field station and museum. The headquarters is now located along Bolinas Lagoon in Galloway Canyon, owned by Audubon Canyon Ranch.

Seabird research was begun on the Farallones in 1968 and PRBO has been there ever since. In an agreement with the U.S. Fish and Wildlife Service, PRBO conducts research on the island and provides on-site supervision of the Farallon National Wildlife Refuge.

With the coming of Dr. David Ainley from Johns Hopkins University in 1971, PRBO gained one of its most valuable members. For over 20 years, Dave was Program Director of Marine Research. He designed and managed the Farallon research program, which culminated in the book *Seabirds of the Farallon Islands*. An old Antarctic hand, he has done research on seabirds there for nearly 30 years and brought that research under the umbrella of PRBO. His leadership gave the Marine Research program of PRBO direction and national prominence. His presence was a cohesive force for the outfit as a whole, especially a few years ago when PRBO underwent a crisis of identity and was in danger of losing its focus. His dedication to his work and to PRBO were remarkable in these times; while others came and went, he remained. His retiring manner and reticent nature tended to obscure his contributions. (While this manuscript was in the process of being published, Dr. Ainley left PRBO.)

With the advent of its Farallon station and the spread of its ecological interests to the Pacific and Southern Oceans, the focus of PRBO has broadened considerably. Though the attention of this book is centered on the Farallones' ecosystem, the landbird and shorebird programs are also still going strong, the latter under the direction of Gary Page, another longtime staff member. Now that many of the mysteries of bird migration have been resolved, PRBO is busy determining what habitat is critical for the perpetuation of migrating species.

Besides research, PRBO monitors the health of our environment. In this capacity, it provides services of immediate and critical value to our society. Having developed a reputation for scientific impartiality and fairness, it also has begun to play an important role in resolving disputes between commercial and environmental interests by the timely collection and presentation of data at hearings – data that can counterbalance impassioned self-interest and sentimentalism as determinants of public policy. It survives by grants, contributions, programs and memberships.

Los Farallones de los Frayles

for Robinson Jeffers

Monks of the sea,
    wild old men of the current,
among whose bald rocks
    the murre and guillemot,
auklet and puffin,
    petrel and cormorant
burrow and breed,
    monks of the sea,
wild old men of the current,
    gray heads crowned
by coronets of screaming gulls:

Your loins are girt
    with sea lions, seals
and sea elephants,
    and the rolling surf
thunders against your granite thighs;
    old godrocks of the sea,
missionaries of a continent,
    in ghostly cowls of fog and sea spray,
your constant intonations of gull wailing, murre
                  squawking,
    sea-lion barking, and sea-elephant snorting
call the lords of heaven
    to save our planet
             from the dominion of man.

Inverness
October 18, 1978

I

Maiden Voyage

I first went down Tomales Bay in 1970 with Mike Gahagan, then owner-publisher of *The Point Reyes Light*. I had just opened a general practice in Point Reyes Station, and Mike was giving me a tour of the bay when he took me to meet Clayton Lewis, who was rebuilding an old Monterey fishing boat at his shack at Laird's Landing. Clayton fished Tomales Bay for perch, which he sold in Chinatown.

A long green rowboat – Clayton's netboat – and a sailboat lay at anchor off the sandy beach at Laird's. The cove was an old Miwok Indian camp and a beautiful site. Clayton and some friends were working on *Angelina*, and I was immediately taken by her.

Clayton was 20 years older than I and something of a character. Part artist, part fisherman, part boat builder, part naturalist, part jeweler, and part crafts-man, his real passion was the bay. Like a hermit crab, he had found these old buildings uninhabited and moved in, making them his own. Anyone new to the area and interested in the water found his way to Clayton's place.

When I was at the University of California at Berkeley, my wife Barbara and I had come to Drake Bay[1] one summer and seen the salmon fleet. From that day, I had wanted to have a fishing boat of mine anchored there. Years passed while I was in the Army and medical school, but that desire, though submerged

ARTHUR V. FISHER

Angelina at Laird's Landing

in these other activities, was not lost. It began to resurface when I read Steinbeck's *Logbook from the Sea of Cortez* shortly before moving to Inverness. Steinbeck and his friend Ed Ricketts chartered the purse seiner *Western Flyer* to take them on a scientific cruise to the Sea of Cortez. The book made a strong impression on me. Like Steinbeck, I "had no urge to adventure," but to get to small islands, you needed a boat. Adventure comes with carelessness and haste. Learning as I went, I sampled both.

Angelina had been built in Pittsburg, California, around 1920. She had a fine rake to the gunwale and a canoe stern. A classic double-ender, her lines were uncluttered. She had a fishhold and gaff well aft and a cabin midship, which housed an old Chrysler Ace marine engine. The wheel was a used car steering wheel. The house had small windows; a mast in front was flanked by raw wood outrigger poles. Forward was a hatch, with a sliding cover, which led down to two bunks. She had a short carved bowsprit or chicken beak. There was no mistaking her for a yacht.

When Clayton finished the boat, he offered her to me, and I took him up on it. I planned to fit her with gurdies for salmon trolling and to fish commercially on my vacation. But that was before I got involved with PRBO at the Farallones.

We lived in Seahaven in Inverness then, in a house on the bay. Clayton had made a mooring of an old engine, which we dropped 30 yards off our beach, and I kept the boat at home.

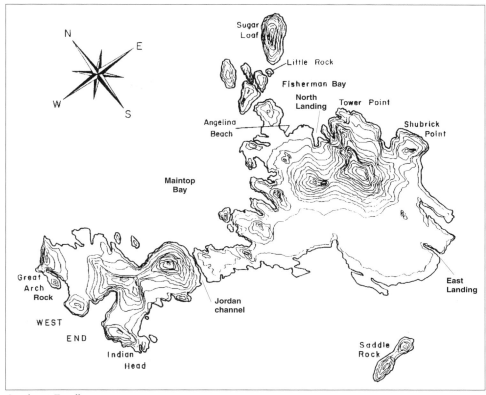

Southeast Farallon

I called the Point Reyes Bird Observatory and offered the services of *Angelina* in transporting personnel and supplies to the Farallones. The director, John Smail, put me in contact with Dr. David Ainley, a new biologist, who said he would call when the need arose. At that time, PRBO was entirely dependent on the Coast Guard for transportation to the Farallones. *Angelina* was the first private craft to ferry PRBO people, groceries and equipment to and from the islands. She was succeeded by the Farallon Patrol of the Oceanic Society (now Ocean Alliance).

Not long after I got the boat, I decided to move her out to Drake Bay in readiness for the trip to the Farallones. I departed midafternoon from my anchorage in Tomales Bay with a light breeze blowing from the northwest. I crossed Tomales bar and turned south at the red whistle buoy, marking the shoal at the tip of Tomales Point, just as the sun dipped into the Pacific. It was my first time on the ocean in *Angelina*. Small seas from the starboard quarter followed me as I ran down past Bird Rock and along the Great Beach of Point Reyes Peninsula. The boat dove and rolled pleasantly, and I took the tiller in the gaff well. Being alone offshore bestirred my senses, and the advance of darkness put an expectant edge on things. I thought of Winslow Homer's painting "Breezing Up" as I lounged back and dragged my hand through the water.

It was dark by the time I reached the old lifesaving station on Point Reyes Beach. The water around the boat was inky and dancing with wave points of light. There was no moon, and the sky was black and full of stars. A ship passed to starboard, its hull barely visible.

Alioto Fish Dock

The light on Point Reyes guided me around the headland. Keeping well away from the cliffs, I looked for the buoy off Chimney Rock. I found the buoy (its light was out) and turned into Drake Bay. The seas soon became flat, and I could see the lights at the fish dock. I ran in among the fishing fleet riding at anchor, happy to be in the company of other boats and in the protective arms of the bay. I couldn't find an empty mooring, so I threw over the anchor and rowed to the rocks near the Alioto Fish Company dock. I dragged the shore boat above the high-tide line and went up to a ramshackle house at the foot of the pier, where Lyla and Lloyd Williams lived. They managed the dock. Lyla, a big, strapping old woman, operated the hoist and tallied the salmon and crabs brought in by the fishermen. A California Indian, Lloyd used to be a fisherman and, during prohibition, a rum runner. Now he sorted salmon and kept the place up.

It was around nine when I knocked on the door. Lyla was surprised to see me coming up from the sea at that hour. She had coffee brewing as usual and put a warm cup in my hands.

I got a call from Dave, whom I still hadn't met, in the fall of 1971. He said the Coast Guard buoy tender hadn't been able to get him on Southeast Farallon; it was either needed elsewhere for buoy repairs or couldn't land personnel due to heavy seas. He had gone out several times only to be brought in again.

Though it was still blowing, I readied for the trip. After three or four days the wind began to slack off. The Coast Guard buoy tender left for the Farallones before I could, so Ainley went with them.

10-29-71 I drove to the fish dock at Drake Bay in the afternoon. Whitecaps were still plentiful, but the wind was not blowing so hard. The weather was clear and the Farallones visible. I rowed out and stowed my gear. As I was getting restless, I thought, why not run out to the buoy and test the water; if it's too rough I'll turn back. I had nothing to lose. So I went to the buoy, and when I couldn't quite make up my mind, I went a little farther, and when I still wasn't sure, I continued a little farther until I was on my way. Dave likened my start to the fledging of a seabird: a little tentative at first.

Halfway to the islands, I began hearing a whooshing noise I couldn't figure out. Being tense anyway, I thought it was the motor. I was looking high and low in the house for the source, when out of the corner of my eye I caught sight of a fin cutting the water. I jumped out on deck and saw several black and white porpoises blowing alongside the boat. At the bow they submerged, circled around behind the wake, and came roaring by again. Hanging to a forestay, I stood on the plunging bow and watched them until they departed. I learned later these were Dall porpoises. On my many trips to the Farallones, they nearly always joined me about midway to the islands. They were like a welcoming committee, and I came to look forward to their greeting.

As I approached Southeast Farallon the seabirds grew more numerous and the rocks loomed larger, becoming in reality the size they had been in my

Fishing boats anchored in Drake Bay

Houses on Southeast Farallon with Seal Rock in background

MICHAEL WHITT

mind's eye. The experience was doubly exciting for a landlubber. Now all I had to do was find an anchorage. I had cruised by East Landing by chance, you might say, several weeks before, but had stayed well off, thinking Dave would be along to show me where to go when the time came to land. Innocently enough, I had taken my mother and wife on a cruise of Drake Bay when gradually I had been drawn to the Farallones by the flat calm. I remember my wife saying as the land receded, "Where do you think you're going?"

On the nautical chart's inset of the South Farallones, I had picked out Fisherman Bay as the best place to anchor, and Ainley had confirmed it. The bay is formed by a line of rocks on the north and the island on the west and south. It had been the traditional anchorage before the mechanical hoist was built at East Landing. Identifying Sugarloaf Rock and passing to the east of it, I entered the relative calm of the little bay, where I dropped anchor on a sandy bottom in 20 feet of water.

My next problem was where to land. At low tide a big surge forms in the channel at North Landing, the obvious choice, so I selected instead a small beach to the west, where the surf was dampened by some offshore rocks. The only drawback here was that the beach and all the surrounding rocks were occupied by sunning California sea lions. I decided to approach slowly and give them time to leave.

I took the shore boat from its place over the forward hatch and lowered it into the water. As I rowed in, sea lions rolled and porpoised in the clear green water around me. Gulls screamed overhead. The abundance of wildlife was thrilling. Here was our Galapagos! (No unique avian species, perhaps, but endemic plant, insect and amphibian ones.)

As I neared the beach, the sea lions seemed oblivious to me. If I were to land here, I had no choice but to go in and see what happened. All at once they saw me, and the beach and rocks emptied of thousands of pounds of lunging, grunting, barking, strong-smelling flesh. The boat rocked precipitously. Then the little beach was all mine.

I jumped into the shallow surf and drew the boat ashore. I hoisted my pack and the boat onto some rocks. I looked out at *Angelina* riding at anchor and knew she would be safe. Already the sea lions were reclaiming their beach.

Least tern

I shouldered my pack and, finding a path, followed it.

The island was a hive of activity. Sea gulls set up a great clamor and stooped on me as I passed. Murres and guillemots dived from the cliffs, and cormorants passed in black lines offshore. The crashing of waves, the bird noise and the barking of sea lions created a din of wild music that filled all my waking hours for the remainder of my stay.

I wasn't surprised to see that no one was around. I figured only Dave and the Coast Guard would be on the island, and I had heard the guardsmen rarely went outside except to raise and lower the flag. I read later where one of them had described duty on Southeast Farallon as "loneliness covered with bird shit."

I came up to two houses and, trying the first, found it empty. Then I went to the second and knocked. Nothing happened for a few moments, then the door swung open very slowly. I was greeted by a surprised Jim Lewis of PRBO, who was still waiting for the *Black Haw*, the buoy tender that was bringing Ainley to the island and returning Lewis home. As the ship could not land passengers without assistance from ashore, and strangers were not allowed on the island, the inhabitants – after a quick head count assured them that all were present and accounted for – could not imagine who was knocking. Jim recognized me because I had treated him for a puzzling rash that proved to be an allergic reaction to Farallon weed, a plant endemic to these islands!

Jim wanted to see where I had stowed the rowboat to be sure it was safe from the big ground swells that broke around the island; after that he led me on a quick tour of Southeast Farallon. The first place we visited was a sea cave with a beautiful tidepool carpeted by red and royal-purple sponges and full of red and green anemones, deep purple urchins and sea worms. The visit to the cave was, I felt, my initiation into the mysteries of this extraordinary island.

When the *Black Haw* arrived and Dave Ainley was lifted up on the Billy Pugh, I finally made his acquaintance. Lewis and landbird biologist Dave DeSante departed, the latter telling Ainley of a South Polar skua he had seen that day. Venus was low on the western horizon as Dave and I walked back to the house.

Early in his college career Dave had flirted with being a medical doctor; but after studying birds for a summer on Kent Island in the Bay of Fundy and learning that you could make a living at it, he threw over medicine for ornithology. Graduating from Dickinson College, Spencer Baird's *alma mater*, he enrolled in a Ph.D. program in ecology at Johns Hopkins, obtaining his doctorate in the quick time of 27 months, 12 of which were spent in the field in Antarctica and Alaska.

Beginning college as a petroleum engineering major at the University of Texas and continuing at the University of Oklahoma, I had switched to English after transferring to Berkeley for my last two years. After a hitch in the Army, I had returned to medical school at the University of Texas in Galveston, where I started watching birds. It happened almost by accident; a friend gave me a pair of field glasses, and training them on a bird (a yellow-billed cuckoo), I was hooked. Some days, dressed in my white smock, I stopped at the marsh on my way to class and stayed until evening. (I had a lot of catching up to do!) This activity changed my life. (Outside my studies I was adrift, reading all the great books and drinking too much, looking for something I couldn't quite identify.) For the first time, I was put in touch with the natural world on its terms. Whereas I had once viewed a beach as only a place to body surf and unused land as vacant, I now came to the realization that these places were used by other species. Open space was necessary to support their life cycles. (And our life wasn't all that much different from a bird's or mammal's. It, too, had cycles and seasons and biological rhythms, if only we could turn down the brain long enough to experience them.)

I also experienced my first sense of environmental loss on Galveston Island. In my senior year, I had found breeding colonies of least terns and black skimmers on the West End. Barbara and I had first become attracted to the little terns when, during courtship, the gallant males brought tiny fish to their mates waiting on the pier of the fish camp where we lived. On their breeding grounds, the bantam birds vigorously defended their nests by screaming and diving at intruders, delivering a painful blow to the head with their sharp beaks.

The black skimmer, more retiring than the feisty little tern, tried to decoy its enemies – rattlesnakes, foxes, coons and humans – with the broken-wing display. Trolling its lower mandible in the quiet water of evening, the elegant bird left a softly rippling wake as it passed. Watching it at the end of day, I felt as though it were the bearer of peace, the messenger of sleep.

These were the first seabird breeding grounds I had visited and were places of considerable power; I naively expected they would always be there. But the tern's belligerence couldn't save it, nor could the skimmer's feigned injury.

When we returned to the island several years later, a bridge to the mainland had been built on the West End, and we couldn't find the nesting colonies of terns and skimmers. The bridge, connecting the uninhabited end of an island with a sparsely settled section of coast, was hardly necessary; it was built because it could, not because it should be built.

My preparation for the sea – this motoring about the fringes of it – had been sketchy. I spent a short period during my high-school years in Corpus Christi, Texas, in the Sea Scouts. I went on only one cruise with the troop. We spent all morning down in the cabin eating green-frosted cupcakes waiting for a storm to pass. Finally sailing in the late afternoon, we hit bottom just outside the break-water and lost our centerboard, which we could not retrieve. While the boat wallowed in choppy seas, we took turns at the gunwale throwing up green vomit, which matched the color of our faces. What I recall best about the episode, however, was not the seasickness but the phosphorescence flickering strangely about our feet and legs as we waded ashore late that night. A similar luminous quality has distinguished most of my field experiences, no matter how uncomfortable they might have been.

Peregrine falcon

FJW

My only other experience in a boat larger than an outboard occurred when I was still at Berkeley. I remember the day well: the House of Representatives Committee on Un-American Activities was holding one of its first hearings in San Francisco. When the invitation to go sailing came, we relinquished our plans to go to the hearings and went on the bay instead. Though my interest in politics was at its peak and I really didn't care much about sailing, I made a choice I understood only later.

The boat that day was a 40-foot ketch or yawl, and we had to come about in a heavy swell under the Golden Gate Bridge. Looking up at the span high above the water, and down at its steely shadow cast on the waves, I was left with the impression that it was somehow a barrier to my "inland soul," that it would be dangerous for me to venture beyond. Later we dropped anchor in Sausalito and rowed ashore for martinis.

10-30 I helped Dave build what is now called the cormorant blind. We explored West End, Raven Cliff, Indian Head and Great Arch Rock. (There is a fine portrait of the latter by Albert Bierstadt in the DeYoung Museum in San Francisco.) The West End is the weather side of the island, and big swells thunder continuously against the cliffs and roll in great booming breakers up the surge channels choked with huge logs and sea wrack. We crouched on the rocks and watched through the air hazy with mist as the wave tops were illuminated by the setting sun. Southeast Farallon is the last outpost of the North American continent in the middle latitudes, its blinking light and droning horn the last utterances of man before the silence of the Pacific Ocean stretches westward 2,000 miles to Hawaii.

10-31 As Dave had never been there, we took *Angelina* to the North Farallones, seven miles distant. It was an unusual day: sunny, warm and so calm that Dave could have stepped onto the largest island from the bow of *Angelina*. H. H. Bancroft in his *History of California* mentions in a footnote that a Russian family and 23 "kadiaks" were found living on "the North Farallon" in 1825. (It is hard to imagine where they would have made camp.) We saw two peregrine falcons, one eating an auklet on a rocky pinnacle. There were many sea lions on the northernmost rock. These islands are spectacular on a clear day, rising pyramid-fashion from the deep-blue sea and ringed at their base by white foam.

When we returned to Southeast Farallon, Dave stood his daily sea watch at the spotting scope, identifying and counting the birds that passed. Every night, as was PRBO custom, we listed what we had seen in the daily log, the *Farallon Journal*. One of our first entries, made the day we arrived, was of a northern shrike eating a winter wren, the northern shrike being an island record, i.e., never before seen here. Another highlight was a spectacular aerial display by an adult peregrine falcon over Shubrick Point. It dashed, spiralled,

Western gull

stooped and rose precipitously on the updraft; then it perched nearby, sporting its rakish sideburns, which serve to diminish glare like lampblack below the eyes of a ballplayer.

I had my first view of Cassin's auklet, a small bird slightly larger than an American dipper. (John Cassin was Curator of Ornithology at the Academy of Natural Sciences in Philadelphia in the mid-1800s, the heyday of American ornithology.) The most numerous inhabitant of the island, yet often unseen by daytime visitors, Cassin's auklet spends the day at sea and returns to its burrow on the island only under cover of darkness. Bright moonlight is enough to keep it offshore. Nicknamed the Farallon peeper, it hops around on the ground like a frog – and sounds like one, too. Crawling with auklets, the island after dark reminded me of a southern swamp.

STEVE MORRELL

California sea lion bull

Other birds on our list, many of them new to me, were ancient murrelet, tufted puffin, pelagic cormorant, black-legged kittiwake, wandering tattler, whimbrel, fulmar, sooty shearwater, ashy storm-petrel, red phalarope, brown pelican, short-eared owl (it flew out of a sea cave), burrowing owl, black oystercatcher, golden plover, water pipit and golden-crowned kinglet. Also noted were two small groups of elephant seals, back from the brink of extinction, one at Sand Flat and the other at North landing, Steller (northern) and California sea lions, and one harbor seal.

Seabird ecology was still in its infancy, and I bombarded Dave with questions. As he was very laconic and often seemed lost in thought, it was one way to initiate conversation. And with all the unanswered questions, small talk seemed intrusive. Though words offered few insights into Dave's character, his smile was an open window into his personality.

Tramping over the island, hypnotized by the swell billowing the blue-gray expanse of sea and by the easy soaring of gulls, I glimpsed the larger world that we lose sight of in our narrow pursuits. I had also come down with islomania, which Lawrence Durrell in *Reflections on a Marine Venus* describes as "a rare but by no means unknown affliction of the spirit.... The mere knowledge that they are on an island, a little world surrounded by the sea, fills them with indescribable intoxication. These born islomanes....are the direct descendents of the Atlanteans, and it is toward the lost Atlantis that their subconscious yearns throughout their island life..."

11-1 I took leave of Ainley on a foggy morning. Halfway to the mainland, I exited from the tenebrous fog into the sunlight. The sea reflected the change by turning smooth with big swells that slowly rocked *Angelina*. Time seemed to drowse and anxiety slept.

In the early afternoon I reluctantly passed under the span of the Golden Gate Bridge and then through its steely shadow, approaching now from the other side, no longer barred from the ocean. I tied up near Fisherman's Wharf at Boicelli and Mercury Marine Supply, one of the last vestiges of reality at that famous location. Barbara was there to meet me.

11-2 We departed for the Sacramento – San Joaquin River delta, touring

San Francisco Bay on the way. We cruised, if you can use that word for this boat, to the south bay and around Yerba Buena Island, back and forth under the silver span of the Bay Bride past the freighters anchored out. Most of the freighters were unloaded and stood tall in the water, increasing our sense of being Lilliputions among giants, which was later intensified by passing them in the narrow confines of the river system. We made it only as far as San Pablo Bay, where we threw over the anchor near the east shore.

11-3 At first light we got underway, turning into the Carquinez Strait past the sugar mill to the town of Crockett. Anchoring outside the road near the shore, we rowed in for breakfast. A chain-link fence to keep people off the railroad tracks blocked our way. Climbing over it, we found a restaurant.

After breakfast and a walk around Crockett, we motored into Suisun Bay, where we encountered a large flock of the lovely little Bonaparte's gull in its winter plumage with the large blackish beauty mark behind the eye, a remnant of its summer hood.

We cruised past the islands bordering the bay and saw many black-shouldered kites and short-eared owls. In the afternoon, we explored Cache Slough, which was filled with duck blinds and decoys, and anchored far up the slough near a dyke. Mallards were streaming over the dyke and into a field we couldn't see. Taking the shoreboat, I rowed in, crawled up to the edge of the dyke and peered over. The ground was covered with mallards waddling and tumbling over the stubble. I felt like I had entered a time machine and I was a boy again, spying on the true bounty of our country. I lay there looking until it was almost dark.

A beautiful autumn evening; we cooked out on the deck of the boat and sat talking until late.

11-4 We backtracked to the San Joaquin River and, with our charts close at hand, explored the maze of islands in its delta as far as Stockton. Without them we would have been lost in no time. Returning to the Sacramento River, we headed upstream, stopping at the town of Courtland to eat. After taking on fuel at Freeport, we got into an argument because I would not stop and it was getting dark. Just past the Freeport Bend where the river swung back to the north, I cut the corner and we felt a terrible thud and the boat went out of control. I was in the gaff well steering and, looking over the stern, could see that the rudder was missing. Rushing forward to cut the throttle and throw over the anchor, I stopped the boat in its lazy spin back down river. We had hit a wing dam, and it had neatly plucked the rudder from its frame. Luckily, the ship channel did not follow the river here so, leaving our running lights on, we went below to bed. We would have to wait until tomorrow to figure out what to do.

11-5 After coffee, a solution presented itself. I had on board a large oar or sweep that Clayton had given me, for what purpose I don't recall; perhaps it was to be used like a pole or a paddle. Anyway, putting Barbara at the throttle, I stood on the rear deck and put the sweep over the stern to use as a rudder, and we began to make our uncertain way upriver. Things went faily well until we got closer to Sacramento and encountered Sunday boaters and more drawbridges. When we did not yield the right-of-way, the boaters would whirl around us in their powerful craft hurling insults and obsenities in the direction of the bearded boatman and his wife, which made me angry and Barbara more nervous.

Drawbridges were another challenge. As we had outrigger poles and a mast with radio antenna, all the drawbridges had to be raised for us. They are slow to rise and it was difficult to hold steady in the stream when we couldn't maintain headway. I would blow a blast or two on my horn – an old hand-held galvanized metal foghorn – as far in advance as I could and still be heard. Then began the agonizing wait until the siren went off and the bridge began its painfully slow rise. Sometimes, we had to make a circle if we had gotten too close, which was hard to do in the current of the narrow river.

We finally threaded our way through the pleasure boats, freighters and drawbridges to Sacramento, pulling into a boat works in the town of Broderick just below the Sacramento's junction with the American River. We tied up alongside another old boat, which was being restored by its young owners for ocean fishing and a life of adventure.

11-6 We met with the owner of the boat works, an obliging fellow, and he put the boat on the ways and took measurements for a new rudder, which he said would be ready later that day or early the next morning. Amazingly, there was no other damage.

We took the bus into Sacramento and, having nothing better to do, visited the chambers of the State Assembly and the Senate, where nothing much seemed to be happening, either. Afterwards, we wandered around the Capitol grounds, bought a yellow rain slicker and found a good book store. Perhaps I sensed that inclement weather was in the forecast.

11-7 There was a delay – as always in the matter of things pertaining to a boat – in getting the rudder and, as Barbara had to get back to meet her father, she left on Greyhound for the coast. I invited the couple that we had tied up alongside to return to Drake Bay with me. We did not get away until late afternoon, just as the first winter storm blew in. Finding a pier down river, we tied up for the night, and I let them have the bunks below. I spread my sleeping bag on deck, hoping it would not rain before dawn. Sometime in the night it began to pour, and I had to go below with my guests.

11-8 When we awoke, or rather got up, for I don't think anyone slept, the weather was clear and windy. We cruised merrily along until we hit Suisun Bay. I could see that the open water was churned into white caps by the brisk winds, but I naively thought that inland waters would present no problem for a 27-foot Monterey fishing boat. It was, as they say, a rude awakening. The shallow water and steep waves with their short period subjected *Angelina* to a severe pounding as she beat into the wind. I finally ran for cover into the "Mothball Fleet" of decommissioned Navy ships anchored in ranks near the west shore. In the long avenues between the rows of ships, the water was calmer and we "huddled down" to wait for the wind to subside. The empty lanes of water and the tall ships gave one the deserted feeling of the Financial District on Sunday. The wind slacked off a bit at dusk, and we ran across the entrance of Carquinez

Strait to a yacht harbor at Martinez. Finding a berth, we tied up for the night, but due to the small craft warnings the harbor was empty of people, and we could not climb over the locked gate to get something to eat, so we made do with what little we had on board.

11-9 Weather sunny and calmer with big puffs of cloud. As we came through Raccoon Strait and into the vestibule of San Francisco Bay, we encountered gale force winds. Small craft warnings were out at the Corinthian Yacht Club. As I neared the Golden Gate I became determined to reach Drake Bay that night, small craft warnings or no. We had no more food, no place to tie up and anchoring out was not a welcome thought.

We passed under the Golden Gate Bride in the early afternoon, hugged the north shore to Point Bonita, turned into the Bonita Channel inside Sears Rock to avoid the Potato Patch and headed north. A rough go, but *Angelina* never missed a beat.

I knew I had to give Duxbury Reef at Bolinas a wide berth, but in my optimism I at first mistook it for Point Reyes because I could see no promontory beyond it! No harm was done, for I soon realized my mistake, but it was discouraging. The going was agonizingly slow, pounding into every sea head on, the spray gusting over the cabin and blotting out the view ahead until the one small wiper could sweep clean the tiny pane of glass I was straining to see through.

As we neared Duxbury Point, I swung the boat back to the south to avoid the reef. Finding the buoy, I gave it a wide berth and headed toward Double Point. As the afternoon turned quickly to evening, it was brought home to me how far we had yet to go. We were battling wind and current and probably the tide as we lurched slowly toward our destination, now visible on the horizon. Conversation grew less as night fell and the little boat continued to labor without, it seemed, making much progress.

It was dark as we passed Double Point and entered Drake Bay, which had never seemed so large as it did tonight. When I had entered it at the beginning of this trip, it had seemed like a haven; now it was the last hurdle. But the lights at the fish dock, twinkling orange in the blue-black night, beckoned us on.

Gradually the seas became calmer as we entered the lee of Point Reyes, and crab boats began to materialize out of the night. I brought the boat up to the pier and the young woman scrambled to safety, hardly touching the ladder, it seemed, on her way up, and the two of us went back to try and pick up the mooring. After several attempts, my companion caught the painter with the boat hook, and we made the mooring line fast. But we were not quite home yet. Bucking a strong offshore wind, we rowed in to the pier with considerable difficulty.

Lyla Williams made fresh coffee while we waited for Barbara to come for us. When I walked out to the car, I seemed to be thrust off the ground with each step, floating slowly back down as I advanced, my body still traversing the hills and valleys of the sea. I could not release my grip on the wheel until I had had two or three martinis at my friend Vladimir's restaurant.

II

Tomales Bar

Bred as we, among the mountains,
Can the sailor understand
The divine intoxication
Of the first league out from land?

Exultation is the going
Of an inland soul to sea,–
Past the houses, past the headlands,
Into deep eternity!

Emily Dickinson

The *United States Coast Pilot* gives this description of Tomales Bay: "[It] enters the southern part of Bodega Bay eastward of Tomales Point, and extends southeastward for 12 miles with an average width of 0.5 mile. The channel with depths of 4 to 8 feet is marked by buoys for about 4 miles to deeper water inside the bay. The entrance bar is dangerous and should not be attempted by strangers. A 6-knot current may be encountered on a spring tide at the entrance to the bay." So-called sneaker waves occur on the bar and can capsize any vessel they encounter. They are most apt to occur in calm weather, on an outgoing tide, when a big swell is running. Breaking waves occur routinely when the wind is fresh out of the northwest, but then they don't merit the title sneaker wave. I came to prefer Drake Bay to Tomales Bay as an anchorage, not only because Drake with its white cliffs is a strikingly beautiful place, but because a boat can be trapped in Tomales Bay by wind and tide.

Tomales Bar (between headland on left and buoy on right) on a calm day. Bodega Head in background.

Many boaters have lost their lives on the bar, not a few of which were old-timers with lots of experience in these waters. Many others have survived accidents here. If you cross Tomales Bar at the wrong time, or enough times, you are bound sooner or later to be troubled.

3-4-72 With an OK from Dave Ainley, the poet Robert Bly and I picked up the anchor at Seahaven in the late afternoon and set out for the Farallones. Dave and I agreed that a man of letters might benefit from his experience of this rocky nursery, which in its wild profusion of life matched any creation of the imagination. Only one poet, Milton Ray, in a book of poems published in 1934, had cast the islands in his poems. His book was long out of print.

I had met Bly when he was living in Inverness. My nurse, a relative of his by marriage and knowing that I was interested in poetry, had gotten us together. As he had none of the stuffiness of Harvard where he had gone to college – and where the egos produced are oftentimes bigger than the minds – we got on well. He had since returned to his home in Minnesota and was out here on a reading tour when I asked if he wanted to go to the Farallones. On the day of our scheduled departure, he was late and didn't arrive until midafternoon. I had been wanting to make a night cruise to the islands, and now was as good a time as any.

We reached the bar just as it was getting dark. The tide was going out, and the breeze was fresh out of the northwest. In the failing light, I had difficulty seeing whether the bar was calm or breaking. As I could see the gong buoy silhouetted on the horizon, and it did not disappear in the swell, I concluded the bar was flat and we could make it. Aroused by the elements, I steered toward the open water of Bodega Bay.

Bly stood on the fishhold hatch, looking over the house. I remember the first breaker, but at the time I didn't believe it. The bow of *Angelina* was thrust rudely up as a ragged crest of water slid under the boat. The bow crashed into the trough. I looked wistfully back at the wave as it broke into surf. Turning toward the inevitable, I saw the second wave, bigger than the first. I shouted to Robert, "The bar is breaking." In addition to fear, an exhilarating incredulity gripped me. Again the bow swung sharply up as the 27-foot boat reared on its skeg. The snarling wave crest passed under us, and the bow fell with a shivering thud into the hollow left by the racing wave. When I looked ahead and there was no third comber, I relaxed my grip on the wheel and released a long breath; we had made it intact across a breaking bar. When we tied up at Bodega, we saw that the anchor had been flung from its resting place on the bow back to the house.

At the whistle buoy, we wore away toward Southeast Farallon. Then I noticed water was slopping out of the bilge, and the automatic pump was not working. When the floorboards began to float, I decided to come around and go for Bodega Harbor. Robert began furiously working the hand pump. For a moment I wondered if we hadn't sprung a plank.

I could see the silhouette of Bodega Rock looming dark against the starry sky and figured the harbor entrance must be landward of it. I found the opening and followed the channel markers past Spud Point and around to the east side of the harbor. The reflections of onshore lights shivered in our wake as we glided through the empty channel. We tied up at the Tides Fish Company dock.

An elderly man with a little mustache and a white tab of whiskers on his chin approached me as I stepped off the boat. He introduced himself as Swede Anderson. He said he was an amateur boat designer and praised the classic Monterey lines of *Angelina*. He asked us our destination and when I told him the Farallon Islands, he warned us about the shoal to the south of Bodega Rock where he had seen a sailboat rolled completely over by big seas. When I told him about our narrow escape on the bar and about our anchor being tossed back to the house by the breakers, he admonished us with a story about a similar occurence where the anchor went overboard and held the boat on the bar until it broke up.

Sobered by Swede's stories, we moved to Shaw's Marina, where we found a berth for the night. We walked up the hill to a little cafe for a late supper. While we ate, Robert told me of a theory he had read somewhere that animals were more mature as a species than humans because they could each obtain their own food and did not require clothing or artificially heated homes to survive.

We slept ashore. In the morning we were accosted by a grizzled old fisherman. He had leased his fishing boat to two fellows who wanted to go for tuna, and they had never returned. The boat was his most valuble possession and now it was gone. Although eager to cast off, we listened sympathetically as he sputtered and swore. Perhaps he thought we might come across it, I don't know. Finally he let us go.

The wind was calm, and we could still make the Farallones.

3-5 We cleared the jetty shortly after daybreak. The water was quiet and the weather clear, but we were careful to avoid the shoal Swede had told us about. Gray whales with their barnacle-encrusted hulls rolled and blew in Bodega Bay. Hundreds of murres fed and rested in small groups. We saw a few rhinoceros auklets off Point Reyes Beach. Farther out, we began seeing fulmars gliding stiffly over the fringe of the seas. Many kittiwakes floated about. Suddenly Robert shouted that more whales were nearby. The blowing Robert heard was from a pod of a dozen Dall porpoises that had come alongside. We both went forward and hung onto the forestay to watch these magnificent black-and-white mammals until they tired of playing with *Angelina* and swam away.

Later we passed near a raft of sea lions dozing on the surface. Bunched together, they resembled a tangle of kelp. Taking alarm at our proximity, they awakened into sleek swimmers porpoising through the water in their hurry to escape. A superlative day at sea.

Tower on Southeast Farallon and Maintop on West End appeared first, like two rocks disembodied, floating above the haze. Gradually Shubrick Point and the Hesperian Pinnacles came into view, then Great West Arch. As we neared the islands, we noticed they were a lovely yellow-green hue from the Farallon weed, which was at its luxuriant peak. Nesting cormorants and gulls would later strip the island bare, when it would again assume its austere gray color. But now the usually somber rocks rose like a tropical isle from the sea. We passed the island to the west and circled back to Fisherman Bay, where we dropped anchor at 11:30 A.M., five-and-one-half hours after clearing the jetty at Bodega.

Tomales Bar breaking

MICHAEL WHITT

California sea lions

The ursine chorus began a rousing chant at our arrival. Several sea lions dived into the water to greet us, poking their heads up near the boat and barking. The California sea lion bull resembles a grizzly bear with its high forehead and large hump. The Steller with its flatter face and light pelage appears akin to the polar bear.

We landed on Angelina Beach where I had come ashore on my first visit. It is part of what has since been named Dead Sea Lion Flat, but the only sea lions I ever saw there were very much alive. Dave was waiting for us and helped haul the shoreboat upon the island.

After lunch Robert went up for his nap! We only had a few hours of daylight remaining before tomorrow's early morning departure, but we could not persuade him to join us for a tour of the island. It had been an intense 20 hours, but Robert never mentioned our near mishap on the bar.

After putting the finishing touches on the cormorant blind, Ainley and I went over to Maintop, crossing Jordan Channel, the narrow rift that divides it from Southeast Farallon, in a boatswain's chair. Buffeted by the wind, we sat on Indian Head and watched the murres come in to roost over the boiling waters of a surge channel. On the way back, we stopped at Raven's Cliff, where a pair of ravens used to nest. A lighthouse keeper shot them in 1904, because they attacked his chickens. The last report of ravens' nesting was in 1911, when the nest was destroyed twice by the keeper, and the species disappeared for good.

We crossed a vacant breeding ground of Brandt's cormorant, which was strewn with the desiccated carcasses of last year's starved young. It resembled a battlefield, the war having been fought with hunger and neglect. The cormorants lay a big clutch of eggs to take advantage of a peak food supply. When the food supply unexpectedly declines there is a commensurate die-off.

PRBO had designated West End a sanctuary within a sanctuary and does not visit it during the seabird nesting season, so now was a good time to go. Facing the onslaught of the prevailing winds and heavy seas, West End with its high rocks, great arch and steep surge channels is a wild place.

Perched like statuary on almost every rock were western gulls with their red-tipped yellow beaks, snow-white heads and breasts, and gray mantles. Decked out in their finest plumage, they were staking out their breeding territories early.

3-6 Robert and I departed for Drake Bay. We had white water all the way, and spray flew over the house as we beat into head seas. Bly was again on the hatch, with the wind and spray in his face, and was soon drenched. He talked most about Dave's laconism, which was more fascinating to him than the wildlife. It seemed to me that Dave had turned his reticence to good account, and the absence of a need for small talk in his life had peculiarly suited him for field work at lonely outposts in Antarctica and on the Farallones (as it used to be). It also gave him more time to contemplate questions that needed to be asked in his research, and it spared him the temptation to garrulity, which overcomes so many experts. Robert had the gift of gab, and I could see that he was puzzled by an intelligence that had recourse to silence in lieu of speech. He was

Black-legged kittiwake

more interested in the biologist than in the biology. (Perhaps this was a fore-shadowing of the role he was later to assume in the "men's movement.") We hadn't made a birdwatcher out of Robert, and I don't think he ever wrote any poems about the Farallones.

Robert was reading at the University of California at Santa Cruz that night. As soon as we got back to Drake Bay, we left for the campus, stopping in Inverness only long enough to pick up Barbara and to get Robert a pair of dry pants from one of my colleagues, Ed Kosinski.

III

Elephant Seals

Cruelty has a Human Heart
And Jealousy a Human Face
Terror, the Human Form Divine
And Secrecy, the Human Dress

Blake

*T*he elephant seal or, as it was also known, the sea elephant, was hunted nearly to extinction for its oil. Charles Scammon, an American sealer and whaler writing around 1870, gave the range of *Mirounga augustirostris* as Cape Lazaro, Baja California, to Point Reyes. He added, "Owing to the continual pursuit of the animals, they have become nearly extinct on the California coast, or the few remaining have fled to some unknown point for security." In fact, they were thought at one time to be extinct, until a few survivors were found at Scammom's "unknown point," Guadalupe Island off Baja California.

Victor Scheffer, a U.S. Fish and Wildlife Service biologist writing in 1958, gave the northernmost limit of their geographical distribution as the Channel Islands. In 1972 the first elephant seal pup in over a century was born at the Farallones. In 1981 elephant seals returned to Point Reyes. (What was not fore-

STEVE MORRELL

Elephant seals copulating

seen was the increase in great white sharks in response to the increase in elephant seals.)

In returning to their northern haunts, elephant seals established a large breeding colony at Año Nuevo Island just off the San Mateo coast, where they were easily accessible to study. I went there with Dr. Ainley and his companion Helen Strong in February of 1972. This trip was made in anticipation of the animal's full-scale return to the Farallones.

2-25-72   We drove to Año Nuevo State Park and hiked to the beach for our rendezvous with researchers from the island. Several subadult-male elephant seals were scattered about on the sand like driftwood. Two biology students in wet suits came in a Zodiac for us. Crossing a shallow bar with low breakers, we landed on a tongue-shaped sand beach filled with elephant seals. Trying to avoid the bulls, we picked our way through the resting seals. Whenever we got too close to a bull, it would bellow and rise imposingly on its fore flippers, flopping back down on the sand as we retreated. Stowing our packs in an old wooden building on the windward side of the island, we went out to look around.

Some large shelves of rock to the northwest were filled with California and Steller sea lions. On a lower rock, a small herd of harbor seals lay in their curious rocker or banana fashion, with their head and tail up.

Touring the island we saw many scarred and bloodied elephant seal bulls hauled up in surge channels. These bulls had been defeated in their battle for supremacy on the breeding ground and had taken refuge in these channels to bathe their wounds. During our stay, we would hear at dawn the bulls' trumpet blasts of defiance resonate from the narrow chambers.

Near the center of the island, an old government house with many chimneys and a lovely crust of yellow-green moss on the roof stood abandoned. Its windows broken out and its interior soiled with their waste, it had been taken over by sea lions. They lay on the floor and on the steps leading to the porch. It was now their mansion. (There were many dead and decomposing sea lions on the island from what was thought to be leptospirosis infection.)

Sea lions and fur seals, members of the otariid family, have external ears and an ankle joint that allows them to rotate the foot forward and walk on land. The latter also enables them to assume and maintain an upright posture. They use their fore flippers primarily in swimming. Elephant seals are members of the phocid family, which are characterized, superficially, by the lack of external ears. The phocids, which include harbor seals, are unable to rotate the hind flippers forward in order to walk and must move on land by undulation; they use their hind flippers primarily in swimming. Phocids are usually seen lying flat, though elephant seal bulls rear up to fight and harbor seals sometimes assume a curved attitude when resting. It has been learned more recently that elephant seals can dive to a depth of one mile and stay down there for as much as two hours! No other marine mammal goes so deep.

Flocks of western gulls, the adults immaculate-appearing, dotted the island. Cormorants were perched on low precipices. Turnstones, whimbrels, godwits, oystercatchers and sandpipers poked about in the rocks. A flock of surf birds stood into the wind like statuary, heads tucked under their wings.

I startled an emaciated cormorant resting by a stagnant pool of water with a scum of deep-green algae on it. It held its mouth open and swallowed repeatedly; it must have had something stuck in its throat. It struggled into the sea at my approach. Perhaps the bird had swallowed a fishhook or some other bit of human rubbish.

I saw several elephant seal pups lying alone in coves at the water's edge. Black little urchins, they

Elephant seal pup nursing

STEVE MORRELL

had been born late in the season and now appeared to have been abandoned, at least for the time being. Perhaps their young mothers had left them to join a dominant bull's harem on another beach in order to complete their breeding cycle. The pups' appearance was in marked contrast to the fat, sleek, silvery

Elephant seal bull

STEVE MORRELL

"weaners" (recently weaned young), which were gathered into a creche on the mating grounds.

2-26 Dawn broke clear and cool. After breakfast, we went over to watch the mating of the elephant seals. Dr. Burney LeBoeuf of the University of California at Santa Cruz, who was absent from the island at this time, was conducting a long-term study here of these large pinnipeds. He and his co-workers had marked the dominant bulls for identification with a spray-dyed initial on their backs. The bull was approached from the rear while it rested and the mark applied before the animal, awkward on land, could turn, and lunging, reach the worker. The size, if not the speed, of the two-and-a-half-ton bull made this a sporting endeavor.

The alpha or dominant bulls, with the distinctive nose overhanging the mouth like an elephant's trunk, establish their order of ascendancy by defeating in bluff and battle their lesser counterparts, bulls either too old, too young or too weak to prevail. In battle, they attack each other mainly about their massive necks, the skin of which becomes a thickened, scarred and bloody shield. The reward for dominance is access to females, groups of which become harems for the victorious bulls. After giving birth to their pups, suckling and weaning them, the cows are ready for mating. Delayed implantation of the fertilized ovum makes conception possible so soon after parturition. For a pinniped, the exigencies of marine existence compress reproduction into a brief interlude.

A description of the scene is worth recording. The alpha bull lies among his drowsing harem. On the outskirts of his seraglio other bulls, usually young males, await an opportunity for a quick copulation. A snort and a lunge in their direction by the alpha bull is enough to quell their ardor, as they flop on the sand in submission. Occasionally an outlying bull captures a female; this usually occurs as the female goes to and from the water. The bull, unable to use his hind flippers for locomotion on land, undulates his huge body across the sand and easily overtakes the much smaller female, who acts as if she were not really putting her heart into escape. The bull flops on top of her, eases off to one side with his front flipper firmly around her waist, and flexes his lower body around her. If she moves, he grabs her with his teeth behind the neck. If the fornication goes undetected by the alpha bull, penetration may last many minutes with what appears to be multiple ejaculations. Between times they lie together, the bull's flipper "lovingly" around the waist of the cow, their breath blowing up the sand before their noses. Their large eyes, used for seeing underwater at great depths, appear at this time to be full of prelapsarian innocence as they watch the lust and carnage around them.

From the time they come ashore and establish their dominance order until mating is over, the bulls must fast to remain in possession of their harems. They do not eat for four months, during which time they are engaged in constant conflict and copulation, most extraordinary circumstances for a fast.

The weaners, lying apart in nurseries, doze as the adults go intensely about their work of perpetuating the species. Flipping sand on their backs to cool off, they await their time of departure from the island.

It is hard not to anthropomorphize the behavior of these animals, but it is perhaps more illuminating to compare human activity to their behavior. A description of human behavior in animal terms might be called zoomorphism, if we bent its meaning a little because, after all, we are created in God's image. In spite of thousands of years of civilization, our animal instincts are readily apparent in modern life. Some animal instincts, such as the relatively uniform fidelity to the rearing of offspring, have undergone attrition in *Homo sapiens*. When the cognitive overlay is stripped away and the rationalizations dissolved, our actions can be appreciated both for what they are and what they are not. We can look at ourselves, for we are mammals, in these creatures without either the rose-colored spectacles of cultural ideals or the dark glasses of unwanted pregnancies, indifferent parenthood, crime and drug abuse, and be humbled as well as amused. (The breeding scene here reminded me of cults and weekend institutions such as Esalen stripped of their intellectual and emotional camouflage.)

Elephant seal bulls fighting

STEVE MORRELL

Descriptions of anti-social acts that involve sexual assault, murder and other repugnant acts often employ the adjectives "bestial" or "animal." These acts are peculiarly human and involve traits and capabilities that animals do not possess, such as envy, greed, jealousy, perversion, intoxication, ideological and religious fanaticism, nationalism and racism. The inappropriate use of "animal" and "bestial" is slanderous to the animal kingdom (in anthropology the same dilemma arises when primitive societies are compared to ours), while zoomorphism sees much animal or instinctual behavior as positive and worthy of study in an attempt to restore to human psychology a balance between instinct and intellect. Animals lead simple, psychologically clean lives compared to many humans. Perhaps intelligence will eventually lead us around to basic and decent modes of behavior before we become extinct, but the way is long and fraught with hazard. If you modify John Donne's line to read, No species is an island entire of itself; every species is a piece of the continent. . . Any species' death diminishes me, because I am involved in animalkind, and therefore never send to know for whom the bell tolls; it tolls for all life, then you can talk interchangeably and comfortably about animals and men in the same breath.

Though it is not helpful to the understanding of animal behavior to anthropomorphize it, human behavior should be included in ethology; in other words, human intelligence and moral precepts do not guide all our actions, though we may explain them exclusively in those terms, and human intelligence is subject to gross distortions that interfere with our basic and good animal instincts, such as the perpetuation of a healthy species that uniformly nurtures its young and does not destroy its environment nor engages in wholesale killing of its own kind. When ethology shifts from populations of animals and birds to individuals and families, then distinctions between animal and human become even more blurred. The curse placed on animals in Genesis, whereby God gave man dominion over them, should be lifted as we near the end of the Second Millenium. Man's neglect and exploitation of animals leading to the loss of species can no longer be sanctified by biblical authority. We should, instead, honor God's covenant with Noah and preserve all species from extinction.

It is the overweening pride of *Homo sapiens* that I am challenging here, not his accomplishments. Man's achievements in engineering, medicine, science and the arts, i.e., the products of the positive application of intelligence and manual dexterity, are wonderful, but where are they leading us? Life is more comfortable and longer, but is it more significant, more profound, or is it less so? Can we ever recover the economy of animal communities or primitive societies, or will we consume and ultimately destroy our planet?

This debate about the relationship of man and animals inevitably brings up the issue of the morality of man's killing of animals. We should accept the ethic of the Native American. Animals can be killed for sustenance, i.e., for food and clothing. They may also be killed for scientific research and predator control, with two provisions: the killing is done with dispatch and respect, and the killing does not impact the survival of the species.

So-called sport hunting is a more complex isssue. If a hunter safety course is required for a hunting license, so should an animal appreciation course be. For example, every hunter of waterfowl should have to learn to identify all prey species in all plumages before qualifying for the hunter safety course. Before you can be a hunter, you must be a skilled birdwatcher. A prospective hunter should also know the breeding biology of his prey, its migratory route and what pressures (loss of habitat, impact of hunting, etc.) affect it. The game should be utilized for food, as it was traditionally. If species numbers are adequate, then hunting should continue, because the hunting instinct is traceable to the origins of life. If the hunter kills merely for sport, without eating the game, then he should shoot at inanimate objects. One should never kill anything simply for sport. When hunting is practiced as a comprehensive experience of the outdoors and not simply as an exercise in killing, it reaches deeply into our collective unconscious and takes on aspects of a quasi-mystical nature.

On the other hand, the overrefined sensibilities of those with the Bambi yndrome should not interfere with proper traditions of hunting, harvesting

Frederick J Watson
Black turnstones

such as the Eskimo killing of northern fur seals, or scientific experimentation. The role that animals have played in the nurturing of our species is an important and healthy one. Only when commercial exploitation is excessive and threatens species with extinction does the hunt become evil, or when the killing is careless. Whaling was not innately wrong, but man in his arrogance and ignorance has threatened the existence of a noble and intelligent mammal that had been his partner in the advance of civilization. Whaling and sealing required courage and the endurance of hardship and introduced man to the wonders of the Arctic and the Antarctic. Antarctica was discovered by an American sealer. The famous ornithologist Robert Cushman Murphy made his first collecting trip to the Southern Ocean and South Georgia aboard a whaling ship.

Nor should concern for animals translate into feeding raccoons on the back porch or otherwise domesticating wild animals and birds. Rescuing young animals or birds when the parents are dead, or nursing back to health certain injured or sick species, may be an exception to the rule of non-interference with wild creatures, though it's more therapeutic for the human handlers than for maintaining wild populations. It can also be useful as a laboratory. Regular feeding of wild birds is such an old and established practice that I doubt that it ever will be discontinued, but it favors those species that have adapted best to civilization, the ones that need the least encouragement. In times of physical hardship, such as a prolonged freeze, man should come to the aid of wild birds and animals.

For those who have difficulty with the logic of a philosophy that sanctions the killing of animals under certain circumstances, while at the same time exhorting society to treat animals with respect and preserve all species from extinction, for them perhaps the theory of complementarity, used to accommodate the wave and particle theories of light, can be useful. In the same way, contradictory urges to kill and to preserve are observed in mankind, even in the same individual. In that sense, they are complementary. Many avid hunters, such as Aldo Leopold was, are in the vanguard of conservation.

If we are to recognize our kinship with animals, then we must accept our instinct to kill other species. No one would dream of making a vegetarian of a peregrine or a puma. Animals rarely kill members of their own species; in that respect, man could learn something from them.

* * * *

At low tide, I escaped from the breeding turmoil of the elephant seals to explore the intertidal zone. The tidepools, the inhabitants of which seem suspended between animal and vegetable life, made a perfect contrast to the elephant seal carnality. There were many chitons on the exposed rocks, including a large black variety which had the intriguing name of black Katy. A large eel waited in the kelp; electric-green anemones waved their tentacles in slow motion and purple sea urchins huddled in their depressions. Small crabs were in every crevice; sea stars, purple and orange, were crumpled into niches of rock and around mussels, upon which they slowly and quietly fed; black and red abalones hid in sea caves. There were fields of mussels and scattered limpets. With the seas calm and withdrawn and the sounds of seal, sea lion and gull wafted away by a gracious wind, I could hear the crabs clicking in their grottos.

IV

Seabirds

At length did cross an albatross,
Thorough the fog it came;
As if it had been a Christian soul,
We hailed it in God's name.

S. Coleridge

4-24-72   To make ready for a trip to the Farallones for the seabird nesting season, I took *Angelina* back to Drake Bay from her anchorage in Inverness. On the way I tried landing on Bird Rock. Turning east at the trees that mark the site of the Lower Pierce Point Ranch, I circled behind the rock, but couldn't land as a heavy swell broke all around it. According to an old report, storm-petrels nested on Bird Rock, and I had wanted to see if they were still there.

Dave and I, in company with Bob Jones of the Museum of Vertebrate Zoology at the University of California at Berkeley, had tried earlier to get on this rock. On the day we chose for the trip the bar was breaking, and we couldn't reach Bird Rock by boat, so we anchored *Angelina* near the mouth of Tomales Bay at Avalis Beach, which is almost directly opposite Bird Rock. We portaged a rubber raft across Tomales Point, and attempted to launch the raft through the surf to reach our goal. The surf was too big, and we finally gave up after the raft was upended a few times. We were blissfully ignorant of great white sharks in those days.[2]

Later in the year, Dave, Helen, her son Craig and I landed on Bird Rock from *Angelina*. A hundred pelicans grudgingly took to the air as we rowed ashore. Guillemots were perched outside their burrows, and many unfledged gull chicks wandered around. We saw several pairs of oystercatchers, and Dave spotted a pile of mussel shells, which usually signifies an oystercatcher nest nearby, but we couldn't find it. Pelagic and Brandt's young-of-the-year congregated on the windward side of the rock. Harbor seals "stood" in the surrounding water and watched, waiting for us to leave so they could haul out again.

Storm-petrels are betrayed by their musty odor, and we sniffed out one occupied nest in a burrow on the northwest side, thereby confirming, barely, that these birds still used Bird Rock for nesting. We found four more old burrows with fragments of egg shells from the previous year.

Today the seas were calm. Many loons were flying. Murres, guillemots, cormorants and surf scoters floated off Point Reyes. A large flock of phalaropes fed around a bed of kelp. A flock of Bonaparte gulls passed in flight. A small, lovely tern-like gull, it is named for a French zoologist, a nephew of Napoleon, who resided in the United States and is considered the founder of systematic ornithology in our country.

The Navy ship *De Steigein* was anchored in Drake Bay. I picked up my mooring near the fish dock and made it fast to *Angelina's* samson post. I rowed in, climbed up the ladder at the end of the pier, and brought up the shoreboat with the hoist. Lloyd and Lyla greeted me with their usual hospitality.

4-25 I drove out to Drake Bay early; when I first glimpsed the ocean just past the RCA receiving station, I could see it was too rough to go out. Two big fishing boats with stay sails set were taking refuge in the bay. I had a cup of coffee with the Williams, the wind buffeting their old house and the radio crackling with static and conversation between the marine operator and fishermen stranded by the weather; then I drove home.

4-26 Clear with a southerly breeze. The same two fishing boats, still rafted together, lay at anchor. Lloyd helped me lower the shore boat. He said it took about an hour to Bolinas, where on the following day I would pick up Dave and Craig and load supplies for the Farallones. Coastal fog was to the east, which obscured Double Point and the Bolinas Mesa, so I set a compass course for the buoy off Duxbury Reef.

The seas were calm, but big, quartering swells from the previous blow were running. Sailing along in the fog, I was completely isolated for the moment. I enjoyed being alone at sea; I was free of responsibility for others, a welcome break from my practice.

Seeing through a rent in the fog the radar station atop Mount Tamalpais directly above me, I realized that, lost in reverie, I had missed the buoy at Duxbury. Reluctantly, I doubled back to Bolinas, for I could have sailed along

MICHAEL WHITT

Bird Rock

like this, oblivious to everything for hours more.

The fog had lifted in Bolinas Bay, and the sunlight glittered on the water. The sand spit at Seadrift lay to starboard, and ahead shone the beach at Bolinas surmounted by a bluff, and above that houses nestled in the greenery of Little Mesa. As I approached the mouth of Bolinas Lagoon, I saw several pink-footed shearwaters and passed a large feeding flock of sooty shearwaters. The *United States Coast Pilot* was no help here, because it did not mention either Bolinas Bay or Lagoon – omissions apparently made due to the insignificance of the harbor.

I had observed the entrance to the lagoon on two occasions from Little Mesa, and Fred Davis, a patient of mine and a sailor from Bolinas, had told me how to enter. I throttled back just outside the low surf that marked the bar at the entrance, and following Fred's directions, I lined the bow up with the houses along the channel and a cypress on Kent Island. When there was a lull in the surf, I opened the throttle and passed into the lagoon.

The tide was cresting, and I got on the beach at Kent Island and couldn't get off. *Angelina* lay on her keel at low tide, high and dry. When the tide came back in after dark, Ed Letter kindly came down and helped me kedge her off the sand. We tied her up at the Bolinas Rod and Boat Club.

I should say a few words about Ed Letter, the unofficial harbor master of Bolinas Lagoon. He operates a small boatworks at the head of the shallow lagoon. (His works can only be reached on a spring tide.) He was always avail-

Channel into Bolinas Lagoon

able to help any boater with a problem or in need of local information. Though Ed was of an older generation that was, I think, unaware of the dangers of development, his devotion to Bolinas was an essential part of its character. Bolinas would not be the same without Ed.

4-27 Clear. The forecast was for winds to increase to 20 knots in the afternoon with three-to-five-foot seas and three-to-six-foot swells. As Dave and Craig and I loaded *Angelina*, swallows were collecting mud from the edge of the lagoon and daubing it on their nests under the eaves of the Rod and Boat Club. We had to wait for high tide and did not cast off until after 10 A.M. Bumping the bottom only once, we made it out the channel and through the breakers into Bolinas Bay, where we encountered a big flock of sooty shearwaters, probably the same one I had seen yesterday.

At the Duxbury buoy, we wore away to the west and set a course for the Farallones, which were obscured by a silver curtain of fog stretching down from Point Reyes. I got out the direction finder and picked up the Farallon beacon. As a result of the late hour, it became exceedingly rough after we cleared the reef and entered the open sea. The bow slammed into the head seas, throwing out great buckets of water, and pitched over their crests, the prop beating the air. Craig got seasick. As a last resort, I cut the throttle. The fog blocked the sun and the ocean became dark and menacing. We saw several Dall porpoises.

About three hours out, Dave spotted the South Farallones off to port. They were ghostly and barely visible in the fog. Near the islands the seas became calmer, and we bobbed in and made anchor in Fisherman (Tower) Bay. Three puffins were swimming at the mouth of the bay. I always anchored on a line between North Landing and a small rock I called Little Rock, between Arch and Sugarloaf, where the ground is good.

MICHAEL WHITT

A herd of California sea lions were on Angelina Beach and the rocks sur-rounding it. As Dave and I rowed in we made loud noises to frighten them away from our landing, but three big bulls remained on a ledge just above the beach. Dave said he did not want to get trapped on the beach with the bulls. Waving our arms and shouting, we were now surrounded by a barking pride of sea lion heads. The water roiled with their antics.

A screaming coronet of gulls circled above us. Finally we gave up trying to scare the bulls. As we rowed up on the beach, the nearest bull jumped from the ledge and hit the sand beside us with a grunt and a wild side-long glance. The others followed, leaving the beach empty. A thick sea lion smell impregnated the air. Dave took our packs, and I went back for Craig. Then Dave came out in the island Zodiac and helped bring in the gear and groceries.

After lunch, I went up to the top of Schubrick Point to the murre blind, which Dave had completed during the winter. The blind is a covered box that accomodates two observers. There are two peep holes for observing the nesting cormorants, murres and puffins.

Three species of cormorant nest on the South Farallones: double-crested (what was once called the Farallon cormorant), pelagic and Brandt's. The latter are the most numerous and very entertaining to watch.

Brandt's cormorants are colonial nesters. The word cormorant is derived from the Latin *corvus* (raven) *marinus* (marine); Brandt was a German zoologist, who first described this species. The nests are made of Farallon weed and a beautiful pink coralline algae and are just far enough apart to be out of reach of a neighboring bird sitting on its nest. In order to steal nest material from a neighbor, a bird must leave its own nest. This arrangement does not prevent theft, however, but only seems to multiply it. When a bird leaves its nest unat-

STEVE MORRELL

Male Brandt's cormorant displaying

tended, a chain reaction of burglary is set off throughout the colony. The only justice in this comical set of circumstances is that what is gained by theft is lost to theft. I don't know the survival value of this behavior, unless it might encourage the formation of new colonies, but one thing is certain: no nesting material goes to waste! Theft helps conserve a limited resource.

Brandt's cormorants are very formal, old-worldlike birds in their courtship behavior. In breeding plumage they have a lovely, iridescent blue gular pouch, which they expand in greeting and displaying. The male selects a nest site and begins to advertise for a female. He squats and points his beak skyward to reveal his blazing blue gular pouch. The tail is erect and the wings, only partly extended, are fluttered in curious fashion. The beak is lowered to the ground very slowly and then raised again in a ritualistic, highly stylized fashion, a sexual version of a martial arts exercise. The pointing of the beak to the ground seems to say to other cormorants, this is my territory, and to the female, come here and mate with me. The female lands nearby and hops over. Mutual inflation of the blue pouch, billing, grooming and, eventually, copulation, with the male hopping onto the back of the female, follows. With two birds in the household, one goes to feed and gather nest material while the other literally holds down the fort, guarding it from the wind as well as theft. Soon the nest is built and the eggs laid. Single parenting would not work for cormorants or, probably, for any other species of bird.

Murres nest around and among the cormorants, hence the name of the blind. It was the only place on the island that murres could be watched at close range. Indeed, it is one of few such places in the world.

I met Ainley on the way back, and we examined some burrowing owl pellets. We found a mouse pelvis and the wishbone (fused clavicles) of a petrel. We also retrieved from the Helgoland trap a female house finch with what appeared to be a crust of dried berry juice from the mainland on her beak.

4-28 We awoke to the northwest wind shaking the house; the gusts reached 40 knots. I walked to North Landing to check on *Angelina*. The sea was frothy white. The wind made it hard to walk; its gusts stopped you in your tracks. The Monterey, with slack rode, was riding neatly at anchor on the foamy waters of the little bay.

The day was beautiful and brightly scrubbed by the wind. The North Farallones rose starkly from the sea. An escort of gulls circled above me. Guillemots sat on the rocks above the path and issued their high-pitched, keening calls, which reminded me of sounds made by a Moog synthesizer.

I climbed up to the cormorant blind. It is on a rocky prominence above an incline that slopes down to Breaker (Maintop) Bay. The blind faces north, and the prevailing winds blow in your face as you look out at the birds. Cormorants land with coralline algae streaming from their beaks. Appearing momentarily lost, they peer about, shake the algae out of their eyes, fly up, circle and then land at their nest. They can not walk safely through the colony because nesting birds peck them and pilfer their nest material. If a bird drops its material, another bird is quick to appropriate it and tuck it into its nest. When a bird arrives at the nest, there is a formal greeting of nodding and the flashing of pouches. The incoming female, after depositing the nest material, often strokes the male's neck with her beak. Once a male grabbed the female's beak and gave it a hard twist. She hopped over to another displaying male and took up with him. Perhaps she had gotten the wrong nest. Another time, a female, running a gauntlet of threatening beaks, arrived at her nest and was briefly attacked by her mate before being accepted with the usual neck stretching. The male on the nest picked up the challenge behavior from the other birds.

Brandt's cormorants on nest

STEVE MORRELL

I went to the Coast Guard house to hear the marine weather report. Weather for the California Coast from Point Saint George to Point Conception was given at frequent intervals. At every locale wave height, swell size, wind velocity and visibility were reported. Listening to it was informative, even necessary, if you were going out in a boat, but it was more than that, it was like an incantation or a mantra. The magic place names resonated in my mind long after the report was finished: Point Saint George, Trinidad Head, Cape Mendocino, Point Arena, Point Reyes, Farallon Islands, Pigeon Point, Point Pinos, Piedras Blancas and Point Conception. I never tired of hearing these reports which made poetry of the California coast, the sea, the wind and the fog.

Gale warnings were issued for the coast from Point Arena to Point Sur. The wind gauge at the Farallones showed a wind speed of 30 knots with gusts to 40. As this was the first time I had ridden out a gale here, I had some anxiety about the boat, but she remained untroubled at anchor.

I spent the afternoon at the murre blind. (There were only the two blinds at the time.) A tufted puffin had a nest nearby. It stood outside the crevice that sheltered its one egg. The tufted puffin is, literally, incredible looking. Squarish in stature with a large, flattened, gaudy, orange-and-gold beak, it has a white face and orange-bordered yellow eye. Two long, pale-yellow feather tufts curl over its black shoulders. It has bright red-orange feet. Its short stature, hunched appearance, and orange beak remind me of an old New York Jewess, heavily rouged. For some reason, the puffin pair did not incubate the egg, and it did not hatch.

Walking back, I passed many western gull nests. The adults vigorously protect their nests by dive-bombing and pelting any intruders with guano. The birds can strike a person a sharp blow on the head with beak or feet. Evenly spaced like houses in a suburb, the nests usually contain three well-camouflaged eggs that are olive with black splotches. I was told that the gull must have three eggs in the nest; if one is broken or removed the bird will substitute a rock in its place. The gulls commute to the mainland, where they frequent garbage dumps. On my first visit to the islands,

Tufted puffin

Jim Lewis had quickly plucked a bone from the ground and asked me to identify it. When I hesitated, trying hard to think of what marine mammal or extinct bird it might have belonged to, he laughingly announced that it was from a pork chop. Gulls also prey on the unprotected eggs and young of other island nesters. Of all the avian species, the gulls are the hardiest.

One hundred twenty-five molting sea elephants, all weaners and yearlings, were stacked in a little cove to the front of the houses. One yearling had a large scar on the neck, perhaps from a shark attack. They set up a howl when I came near and began to quarrel among themselves.

4-29 Awoke at 5:00 A.M. and the weather was calm, however, not for long. The wind soon came up, but less than yesterday, and made another beautiful morning of crystalline clarity. The full moon was set like an opal in the blue sky. Three big Steller bulls were on the rocks at Sea Lion Cove. They had

DAVID AINLEY

Angelina riding out a gale in Fisherman Bay

enormous manes of coarse hair, thick rolls of fat and blackened teeth and rested in the characteristic pose with head thrown back. A sleek female was draped over the flank of one bull. Another female was being nudged in the flank by a motley pup that wanted to nurse. As I passed, one of the bulls lumbered into the surf.

At North Landing there was a wandering tattler and a small gathering of black turnstones on the rocks. A Heermann's gull stood at attention. The tide was low, and *Angelina* rode quietly at anchor.

Malcolm Coulter, who was studying the breeding biology of the western gull, took me on a botanical tour of the island. Malcolm had published a plant list of the Farallones. We studied the small flowers, mostly weeds, with a hand lens. I prefer wild flowers to their garden counterparts, and tiny flowers under a hand lens are the most beautiful of all. In an Erodium species, clear droplets of nectar could be seen at the base of the sepals. In the corolla of the tiny white popcorn flower, several millimeters in diameter, I saw a flylike insect half the diameter of the flower. On the small, yellow cup of a fiddleneck, a tiny, eight-legged, lobster-colored arachnid crawled over the reproductive parts. We looked for a blue pimpernel, which I had never seen. Malcolm had catalogued it here in the past, but we couldn't find it today. Looking at a gray-and-orange lichen under magnification, I saw a tough-looking green insect less than a millimeter in length pitching over the lichen's fruiting bodies. It had six legs and two black horns on its abdomen. Many large black beetles sheltered under rocks and boards.

I returned to the cormorant blind for another "episode" of cormorant behavior. The scene was quiet without murres; cormorants make hardly a sound. Their communication is all by body language; watching them is like watching a mime troop. The absence of calling focuses your attention on their movements and exaggerates them. Wind, blowing constantly in your face, provides the only accompaniment to their pantomime. Eventually, your nose begins to run and your eyes to tear. Every so often you have to take a break.

4-30 Seas calmer today; no white water. Several tour boats of birders skirted the shore early. By the time Dave and I got started for the North Farallones, the gulf was white-hatched by the crests of sharp seas. *Angelina* was rudely handled by three huge waves off Indian Head, which discouraged further travel, and we put back into Fisherman Bay and dropped anchor.

At mid-morning I went over to watch murres. The Farallones are at the southern extremity of this essentially northern bird's breeding range. The murre fills the same ecological niche in the Northern Hemisphere that is filled by the penguin in the Southern. They even bear a superficial resemblance to penguins. Murres are members of the auk family, the archetype of which is the great auk, now extinct. Like penguins, the great auk was flightless. In pursuing their prey underwater, murres use their wings for propulsion as penguins do their flippers.

Observed at close hand through binoculars, murres are strikingly beautiful birds. On the ocean from a distance, they appear nondescript. They are not black, but a lovely charcoal brown. Beginning at the eye and curving toward the neck there is a subtle line resulting from feather arrangement. The meatus of the external ear is located along this feather line. The inside of the mouth is a bright enamel-ochre. Their color is concealed inside the body as if from a natural modesty. As they squabble on the cliff they not only make a querulous sound, but flash the bright ochre of their mucous membrane like a flag. The hillside is noisy from their clacking.

Tufted puffins

Murres have several distinctive movements. They do lots of bowing, from a mere nod of the head to a salaam. It is often done by two birds as a form of greeting. In walking, they most resemble

Northern phalarope

penguins, with necks outstretched and wings raised. They often rapidly beat their wings, much as a plane revs its engine prior to take-off. They usually nest on the windward side of cliffs, rocks and promontories as they need the lift to get airborn. When the male mounts the female murre, he inevitably beats his wings, perhaps for balance as well as for joy. Murres frequently engage in mutual preening and caressing. One bird points its bill skyward with closed eyes while the other scours its head with little nips of the beak.

Murres are also quarrelsome, as are most colonial nesters – including human city dwellers. When they nest among the cormorants, as they do here at Schubrick, they are constantly backing one other into a cormorant's territory causing the latter to launch a sharp attack on the intruder. The murres settle – for they do not make a nest – just out of reach of a sitting cormorant or, if closer, on another level.

Murres lay one beautiful egg on the bare rock and incubate it by resting it on the tarsi (fused footbones) to prevent heat loss. The egg is top-shaped and rolls in a circle so it can't be easily lost by falling off a ledge. The single egg is white to pale-green or blue and splotched with black in a unique pattern. It resembles a canvas of modern art on which paint is dripped or thrown. Some ornithologists think this unique pattern makes the egg recognizable to the parents in the overcrowded breeding colony. (Perhaps crowding also plays a role in the genesis of modern art.)

To most sailors – and murres are seen by few others besides birders – murres are the avatars of inclemency: they are birds of the rough coastal waters.

In the afternoon Steve Morrell, a Farallon biologist, and I were witnesses to an extraordinary scene at the cormorant blind. You do not think of birds, except birds of prey, as warriors. Yet in this cormorant rookery, we were to see the most viscious fight I've seen in nature – more vicious than any of the sea-elephant fights on Año Nuevo, although in the latter, much larger creatures were involved. Heavyweights always attract more attention than flyweights.

A cormorant carrying a beakful of coralline algae landed in the nest of another cormorant. Both were presumed to be males. Steve had read in the *Farallon Journal* that two males, unaware of the other, might be building the same nest, and when they chanced to meet, a fight ensued. Based on other observations, I thought that it could also have been a careless mistake on the part of the incoming bird. A bold land grab might also explain it. (I had seen an invading bird prevail in an earlier, much less bitterly contested incident.) Both birds were determined to claim the nest. One got the other's neck in its beak and forced its head to the ground. Then they grappled with their beaks. One then forced its beak down the other's throat. When their struggle drove them into the vicinity of other nests, the sitting birds vigorously pecked the combatants .

One bird was clearly dominant, but the lesser bird refused to give ground. It was hard to be certain which bird was the defender and which the aggressor; I thought that probably the stronger bird was the original possessor of the nest, but Dave felt it was probably the other way around. An animal defending its territory was usually able to repel larger, stronger members of its species. The loser received a beating from all sides. The surrounding birds went for the head whenever possible; we thought surely the loser would be blinded, but its eyes miraculously escaped injury.

The birds remained locked in battle for 15 minutes. Blood streamed over their interlocked beaks. The loser's nuptial crests were blood-stained, and it appeared to be growing weaker. As the vanquished bird began its retreat, the victor attacked from the rear. The loser rallied and grasped the other's neck, using its beak like a surgical clamp. But the rally was short-lived, and the stronger bird resumed its assault. Finally the weaker bird struggled to a rock about six feet distant, where he stood, bloody, his wings hanging helplessly open, coughing and panting.

When I left 45 minutes later, the ousted bird was still standing on the rock. It seemed to have recovered a little and had even tried its wings weakly, but it remained grounded, its crests bloody, its beak now sheathed under its folded wing.

I think more can be learned about human behavior by observing animals than is learned from social studies, which are encrusted with so much cultural and contemporary bias that results are confusing and often contradictory. Max Planck, the German physicist, has suggested that the study of brain function is inherently difficult, because it cannot be studied except by another brain. In the same way, but to an even greater extent, the prejudices, premises and presuppositions of the social scientist interfere with an objective study of his fellows' behavior.

On the way back to quarters, I accidentally stepped on an auklet burrow and caved it in. When I excavated the dirt to see if it was occupied, an adult auklet escaped under my hand and went into another burrow. I retrieved the egg, and after inspecting it to see that it was intact, I replaced it in its cul de sac. I reconstructed the burrow with a board, which I covered with dirt. I checked later in the day and the egg was there, but not the adult. Worried that the embryo would die from cold, I returned at sunset to find the egg gone, too! I removed the board to see into the burrow: no signs of disturbance, no pieces of egg shell, nothing. I don't think the adult could have moved the egg. Even if it had tried, I don't think it could have been successful in daylight with gulls all around. A marauding gull could have gulped the adult whole and carried the egg off, leaving no trace of what happened at the site of the burrow. Perhaps a gull saw me check for the egg before, and after I left, it somehow managed to reach in and steal the egg, though the burrow was quite long and narrow. I didn't have the wrong burrow, as I had marked it and been back to check it once before. It was strange.

In the evening, I helped Dave dissect an ashy storm-petrel. We identified the supra-orbital glands, which remove excess salt from the circulation, enabling the birds to drink seawater. The salt is discharged through the tube-nose. The tiny lungs are an unspoiled pink without any taint of anthracosis, the black pigmentation that occurs in human lungs from inhaling cigarette smoke and breathing foul air. The trachea and carina (bifurcation of the trachea) are so delicately wrought that even a confirmed evolutionist could almost imagine the hand of God. The skin is a transparent membrane through which the muscles and viscera are visible.

Malcolm Coulter found a reference on sexing live petrels and read to us that sex could be told by the size of the vent. Vent: there is even a poetic, airy word for anus!

5-1 May Day: what better place to celebrate it than here! Dave and I arose early and took *Angelina* to the North Farallones. The sea was rough, and the trip took more than two hours of steady pounding. The waves had a very short period and came from all directions, conditions the fishermen refer to as "slop."

Middle Farallon was almost completely awash; a few cormorants loafed on top of the rock, just out of reach of the waves. Near the first islets of the North Farallones, the motor died from condensation in the fuel line. (Yesterday it was a hermit crab in the water intake!) I shouted to Ainley to make a sea anchor of some fenders in the fish hold and throw it over so we wouldn't slip into the trough of the heavy seas, but the motor restarted straightway. Dave was an

Adult Cassin's auklet

MICHAEL WHITT

Western gull eggs hatching

unflappable companion: I never saw him show any fear at sea, and he never got seasick. (Once on a stormy crossing of Drake Passage in the Southern Ocean, he and the captain of the *R/V Hero* were the only two left standing.) His poise was a perfect counterbalance to my volatility.

We saw many sooty shearwaters coursing over the ragged surface of the white water. They are aptly named for their habit of cutting so close to the water's surface that it seems their wings must sever the wavetops. I saw only one auklet, but learned upon our return that Dave had counted 147! A pair of arctic loons in breeding dress passed close enough to the boat for us to see their sleek gray heads and lovely black-and-white-striped necks.

Returning to Southeast Farallon, we were rolled along by the big following seas. I had not completely overcome my fear of following seas and would still rather buck a head sea, because I could see it coming. We passed to the west and south of the island, slipping between it and Seal (Saddle) Rock. We lingered at the mouth of Murre Cave, a high-ceilinged room of rock underneath Schubrick Hill, where several hundred murres were nesting. The cave probably affords some protection from gull predation. There was a continuous stream of murres in and out of the cave.

We anchored in Fisherman Bay and rowed into North Landing. California sea lions peered and barked as usual as we approached Angelina Beach.

After lunch I wandered about the island. At Schubrick Point three puffins skulked, murres bowed and quibbled, and cormorants puffed their blue pouches as they landed. Standing cormorants have a curious hands-in-the-pocket resemblance to slouching men; they use the beak as a hand.

At Sea Lion Cove several large Steller bulls lounged in the Emperor's Bathtub, a natural pool in the rocks that is flushed by the surf. The bulls, weighing a ton, have a thick mane – but resemble bears more than lions. The phylogenetic origin of pinnipeds (sea lions, fur seals, seals and walruses) is obscure, but they are derived from land mammal stock, probably canine carnivores such as dogs and bears. They return to land or ice floes to give birth, breed and rest; most remain near the coast or ice throughout life. When you pause to think about their adaptation to a marine environment, you are filled with wonder at the evolutionary wizardry that makes it possible. Though pinnipeds – pinniped means winged foot, which describes the flippers that are homologous to the feet of land mammals – are not so completely aquatic in their existence as cetaceans (members of the whale family), their amphibious nature is an equally remarkable adaptation.

Sea Lion Cove is an extension of Breaker Bay, the latter so named because its waters are in constant turmoil from the onslaught of the prevailing winds and seas. Sea lions tend to haul out on the weather side for the sake of cleanliness, coolness and insect control. The waters of the cove are often a lovely aquamarine color; tawny sea lions, glossy when wet, swimming through it, present to the eye a scene of extraordinary beauty. The study of natural history is the only field in which the esthetic and scientific rewards are coequal. Here is beauty in truth.

On the way back to the house, I saw a black oyster-catcher, its blunt red beak like an oyster knife, eying me with its beady, red-orange eye.

5-2 Calmer, but the breeze still fresh. Tide low. In the tidepools a dense chaparral of coralline algae was interspersed with large pale-green anemones and colonies of sea urchins. I found a nudibranch.

A kittiwake, named for its call, preened on the exposed rocks.

Steve Morrell and I rowed out to *Angelina* for a trip to the North Farallones, and while not so raucous as yesterday, the sea proved too rough for comfort, so we returned to our anchorage. A huge Steller sea-lion bull was hauled out near North Landing. Its head was thrown back, great rolls of fat encircling its neck. Nature used size to determine dominance before the evolution of man; now we have replaced brawn with brains and bombs.

As we rowed into the beach, the bow bumped a dozing sea lion, alarming it. The alarm spread quickly to its fellows, and soon the water was churned into a maelstrom as the herd made for the mouth of the bay.

We stopped at the cormorant blind, where we had seen the bird fight. Most of the nests were complete now and an air of gentility prevailed at the colony. Only a few unmatched males were still displaying for a mate.

We ate lunch and I slept all afternoon, exausted from the welter of impressions, the wind and the sheer abundance of life here.

After dark we netted storm-petrels. Petrels and auklets feed at sea during the day and return to the island under cover of darkness to escape the gulls. Even bright moonlight is enough to discourage their return. We strung up a mist net on the hill behind the house and played a tape of petrel calls. The moon was new and the darkness was filled with small birds flitting swallowlike through the air: Leach's and ashy storm-petrels. We caught a dozen or so of these small odoriferous seabirds. They silently suffered their fate of entanglement in the net, extrication and imprisonment in the net bag. We carried them down to the house for weighing, measuring and sexing. The ground crawled and the air was thick with auklets, their pale eyes and white periorbital marks flashing like chrome as they passed. The night was clear, and Venus was brilliant in the black sky. As we walked back, I picked out Corvus (*marinus*), Gemini and Corona Borealis.

To me the ashy storm-petrel is more symbolic of the soul of man than the dove. These uniformly dark, downy little birds of erratic flight are rarely seen and nest underground on remote islands, arriving after dark and leaving before dawn. They have a subtle, visceral odor. Hovering over the sea with their legs dangling, they appear to walk on water. From this trait they get their name, which is the Latin diminutive for Peter, who walked upon the surface of the lake of Genesareth. Of perhaps greater interest: the bird was first named in 1703 by the English buccaneer who rescued Alexander Selkirk (Robinson Crusoe) from the Juan Fernandez Islands. In that era only a sailor would have been familiar with the storm-petrel. This little bird is on the wing in storms when the going is heavy at sea, and it is at such times in life that man's soul, or lack thereof, is most evident.

Like a child, I was eager to handle the petrels. They are very docile in the hand. They have a bright black eye, beak and feet. Dave blew up the ventral feathers to find the brood patch, which is bare of feathers, and checked the vent to determine the sex. The birds were weighed, measured and banded. Dropping them into the escape box, we heard them scramble to freedom.

5-3 When I awoke, it was clear and calm with sparkling seas, but soon fog blanketed the island. After the Coast Guard got the Farallon radio beacon working, Dave and I set off for the North Farallones, Noonday Rock and the edge of the continental shelf to look for petrels and auklets. Petrels were rarely seen between the island and the mainland, and Dave wanted to see if we could find where they feed at sea.

A party of gulls followed us as the South Farallones dissolved into the fog. Dave chummed them in with pork rind to decoy other birds. There were many shearwaters, mostly sooty and a few pink-footed. We got many pink-footed to come in close, but though they are great gliders, they cannot maneuver with the gulls for food. They gave surprisingly loud squawks when the gulls plucked the food from under their noses. Both these shearwaters breed in the Southern Hemisphere near Cape Horn and migrate offshore as far north as Alaska during the austral winter. They are burrow nesters, the pink-footed shearwater nesting in densely forested areas! Unlike the albatrosses from the Southern Hemisphere, the shearwaters can traverse the doldrums at the equator.

Fulmars, both light and dark phase, passed in the distance. These snub-nosed, bull-necked, stiff-winged gliders wander over the open ocean from their breeding grounds in the far north. In these temperate-zone waters, seabirds from

LARRY SPEAR

Black-footed albatross

austral and boreal extremes comingle.

We fancied the water got rougher where the continental shelf began and the water depth went from a 100 fathoms to 40 in a short space, but the fathometer on the boat did not measure below 100 feet. It was cold, and the fog began to thicken. A large drag boat, a shadow in the fog, passed off our bow. I was thinking that we weren't going to be able to find many petrels and auklets in this pea soup and that we might as well turn back when Dave shouted, "Albatross!"

I cut the throttle to idle and sprang on deck. Far behind us, emerging from the fog and gliding low over the water, an albatross with its great wing span could be seen approaching *Angelina*.

As the bird drew nearer, the hump on its back from the huge muscles of its shoulder girdle became visible. The black-footed albatross is a pelagic seabird that glides throughout the Northern Pacific from the Bering Sea to near the Equator. These birds leave their nests on the Leeward Hawaiian Islands, Johnston Atoll, the Marshall Islands and To-Shima Island south of Tokyo and wander over the open ocean for three or four years before returning to their natal grounds to find a mate and a breeding site. They do not breed until they are six to eight years old.

The heavy, black beak, armored with horny plates, has a halo of white feathers at its base and there is a stylish white eye mark, giving the great bird an oriental look. The juveniles are sooty brown all over; the adults have white upper and lower tail coverts. An elegant, as well as mythical, creature except in its eating habits and vocalizations.

Black-legged kittiwakes

Two more albatross joined the first. One came to the boat to get the pork rind that Dave was throwing out. When the gulls beat it to the food, the albatross uttered a weak squawk. We passed two or three large flocks of two dozen birds apiece feeding on fish offal in the wake of the drag boats.

The name albatross is derived from alcatraz, which is Portuguese for pelican. Early British navigators must have misapplied the name from reports of early Portuguese voyagers.

We found many Cassin's auklets at the presumed edge of the continental shelf, mostly in small groups of from two to four birds, but we saw no petrels. The smooth, oily surface of the sea, billowed by large swells, was covered with by-the-wind sailors. Large flocks of sooty shearwaters rested among the miniature armada of Velella. A long-tailed jaeger went by far off the bow.

We saw a small, black bird fluttering toward *Angelina*. Was it a petrel? No, just a bronze-headed cowbird lost at sea in the low overcast and fog. It was tired and wanted to land, but the rocking of the boat discouraged it. After making one last pass, it flew off to its fate.

Finding no storm-petrels, we turned for Southeast Farallon. Picking up the beacon with the direction finder, we headed for the invisible island. Soon its vague outline came into view.

As we approached the island, we could see the Coast Guard buoy tender *Black Haw* pumping water to the island. We dropped anchor in Fisherman Bay and rowed into North Landing, where Jim Lewis and Steve Long, recently arrived, were waiting for us.

Later, I saw a dying gull at the site of the old weather station near Jordan Channel. It had been there for several days. The tips of its wings were dyed green from algae in the stagnant pools where it had drunk. Today it could not move, but was still alert. As I approached, the gull rolled its yellow eye toward me. An orange-yellow ring of specialized epithelium encircled the eye, which gulls use to identify their own. I stroked the gull's head, then I withdrew my hand. I was taking advantage of the situation and invading the gull's space. I quickly discarded the idea of taking the bird back to the house, where several other crippled gulls begged for food: it came into the world without my help and it should leave the same way.

That evening Steve Long caught a rufous hummingbird in the mist net. It was an immature male. We counted its heart rate at 1,500 per minute! It was no doubt scared to be in the clutches of Brobdignagians, and that might have stimulated its heart beat a little. Its weight was three grams or one tenth of an ounce! And here it was, lost 25 miles offshore, looking for nectar. Its wings, which buzz like insect wings when it hovers, were quite normal-looking bird wings with comparatively long primaries. Hummingbirds belong to the order Micropodiformes, which also includes the swifts. The bird is classified by its small, weak feet, which tried to grasp our fingers when we turned it on its back.

The hummingbird, like a neuron in the human brain, is an extraordinary form of protoplasm, a rare moment in evolution when a long-shot combination of creative possibilities worked.

5-4 Our time was up on the mythical isles, and we had to return to the real world. The day was foggy; according to the marine weather report, visibility was one-and-one-sixth miles at Point Reyes. Though we had a direction finder, we had to cross the shipping lanes and needed enough visibility to avoid being run down by a tanker.

Yesterday Craig, who was thirteen, found two guillemot eggs, creamy color with dark brown splotches. They had been laid in a shallow crevice in the rock, easily accessible to sight and reach. Like its relative the murre, the guillemot doesn't bother with a nest. The birds are often found in the morning and evening gathered in small groups on the rocks; they resemble informal little chamber ensembles tuning their instruments, which issue a single high-pitched note. The brilliant red mucosa of the mouth flashes when they wail. They also have bright red feet. They are otherwise all black with a bold, calligraphic stroke of white on the wing. They are a singularly stunning in their appearance, a classy bird.

The name guillemot means "little William" in French, and was probably bestowed as a sign of affection. To sailors, guillemots are known as sea pigeons, which they resemble in size and flight.

Craig had found some sea caves on the south side of the island; as the tide was very low, we decided to explore them while waiting for the fog to lift. I hoped he had found Lost World Cave, which is described by Milton Ray in his book. In his notes, Ray states that he was able to visit the cave only on his first trip, as the entrance was blocked thereafter. Dave speculated the cave lies under Lighthouse Hill at the edge of the sea terrace on which the buildings now stand. The cave we explored did not match the picture in Ray's book. As far as I know, Lost World Cave has never been located again.

The larger cave was a lovely purple color with buffy streaks of mineral left by dripping water. The gravel floor was carpeted by white anemones with lavender tentacles and very large red anemones with white tentacles. The lower walls were wainscoted with bright red sponges. There were grand colonies of goose barnacles that grew more colorful the deeper into the cave we penetrated. They had glowing white shells etched with black lines and deep-red lips like sirens. Large, cream-colored limpets studded the walls, and rock crabs, green and red, shone in the crevices. Little piles of a pasta-colored sponge with neat, round holes in it were here and there. A big gum-boot chiton, dull red, suspended between the animate and the inaminate, whiled away its life in the recesses of the cave. Butterfly shells found on the beaches make up the endoskeleton of this semi-creature.

At 11:30 we departed. The sea was, as Lewis said, like a mill pond. We shooed the sea lions off Angelina Beach, and I rowed out to the Monterey. The sea lions cavorted like a dogpack around the shore boat. I rowed back for Craig. I was grateful two trips were required; the bay was so peaceful that I was reluctant to leave.

The trip to Drake Bay was about three hours at *Angelina's* speed of eight miles per hour. Halfway, Southeast Farallon melted into the fog. We passed in front of a tug towing a barge. A Wilson's warbler fluttered up to the boat. It landed once briefly on a shroud and made several more passes before vanishing over the undulating, gray prairie of ocean. That morning another lost soul, a Traill's flycatcher, had been netted at the island.

The direction finder picked up the signal poorly from the Point Reyes beacon. Soon Craig spotted the headlands. As we got closer, we shut down the engine to see if we could hear the horn. We could see the light, and without the noise of the engine we could hear the baleful drone of the foghorn. Now that we could use direct vision, the signal from the direction finder suddenly became clearer.

We rounded the buoy and entered Drake Bay in perfect calm. The beautiful red-orange algae[3] on the cliff faces signaled home. There were many scoters and a few loons resting on the bay. The whistling of the scoter's wings can be heard for long distances over the water on calm days. It is a welcome sound to the sailor. Craig went forward with the boat hook and picked up the mooring line, and we made it fast to the samson post. Putting our packs in the shore boat, we rowed to the dock.

V

Round the Island

I am stucco'd all over with
with pinnipeds and birds....

adapted from lines by
Walt Whitman

*D*r. Chuck Huntington, Dave's mentor at Kent Island in the Bay of Fundy (between New Brunswick and Nova Scotia), was planning a trip to the West Coast, and Dave asked me to take him to the Farallones. Chuck would be on a schedule and didn't have time to wait on the Coast Guard. As *Angelina* was in Tomales Bay, I wanted to move her in advance to Drake Bay, which cut the travel time to the islands by more than half.

7-26-72 *Angelina* had lately begun to ship water from a leak in the shaftlog, and when I boarded she badly needed pumping. While the bilge pump was drying her out, I checked the radio and found it wasn't working. I imagined the following scene: the boat suddenly begins to rapidly take water and is in danger of sinking; I pick up the transmitter to call the Coast Guard and the radio doesn't work. . . Though I was always in a hurry to get going, it was enough to give me pause. After a quick check I found that the wires from the radio were corroded where they joined the antenna, and I clipped and reattached them so I could talk to the marine operator, if necessary. I left my mooring in the early afternoon.

In the bay a large number of brown pelicans – already returned from their nesting grounds in Baja, California – were fishing. The pelicans were accompanied by their mess mates, Heermann's gulls. The gulls eat what the pelicans let drop. Some of the gulls, which also nest in Baja, were still in breeding plumage. A snow-white head contrasted with charcoal-gray back and wings, black tail with a terminal white band, and a deep-red beak make Heermann's one of the two most handsome gulls. The other is the little Bonaparte's gull.

The tide was full when I arrived at the mouth, and crossing the bar in style and slipping inside the red buoy, I ran down the Great Beach to Point Reyes Headland. Small seas and no swells. Why couldn't it always be like this, I wondered idly as *Angelina* gently rolled through halcyon waters. It could if you had time to wait, knowledge of weather, luck and didn't get too far from land.

The day was beautiful, with high, pearl-gray skies and no wind. All along the way there were sea pigeons, murres – both adult and fledglings – and cormorants. I passed close to the large rookery of murres below the lighthouse. On a survey of the breeding seabirds of Point Reyes Peninsula that Dave and I had conducted earlier in the month, Dave estimated the rookery contained more than 3,000 murres.

The water off Point Reyes was aswirl with currents. Whirlpools and small standing waves are generated by the ebb and flow of the tide, as they are at the narrow entrance of Tomales Bay. Even on calm days the water is lively, as though there was a shoal or a large school of fish below the surface. The cliff east of the lighthouse is sheer and filled from top to bottom with pigeonholes resembling boxes in a mailroom. With the coming and going of murres and guillemots, wind and currents, this promontory is always exciting.

Coming into the lee of the headlands, I heard the barking of *Zalophus* – the Latin name of the California sea lion used sometimes by biologists as a nickname. They filled two small beaches and comingled with Steller sea lions (*Eumetopias*) on some offshore rocks. A hundred harbor seals (*Phoca*) were hauled out on a beach near a slotted rock, where Brandt's cormorants nest. The cormorant rookery was crowded with dingy brown young of the year. Farther along, oystercatchers circled and cried as I passed.

The sun finally burned through the fog, and behind the headlands it was warm and calm. Inside Chimney Rock I passed the large tapestries of red-orange algae adorning the cliffs. Drake Bay was beautiful: bright sunlight, deep-blue water and shining white cliffs. A large motor-sailor was unloading salmon at the Cal-Shell dock.

After landing at the Alioto dock, which has since been torn down, I went over to Cal-Shell to see Carlo Crivello, his brothers and friends, who were known as the "Yukon Gang" by the other commercial fishermen. They came up every summer from San Francisco for the salmon season. I met Carlo when I stitched a facial laceration he got from a fishhook. He had taken me salmon fishing on his Monterey, and on that trip I had seen New Zealand (Buller's) shearwaters. The Yukon gang had a big day salmon fishing just off Limantour Spit at the "creek," which was their name for the mouth of Drake Estero.

They gave me a box of salmon and invited me to dinner, but as Barbara was already on her way to pick me up, I reluctantly had to decline the invitation.

On the drive back, I perceived more clearly than ever that this was the first place I had lived that I could call home. The power of this peninsula bred in me a sense of wonder and attachment. And the long reach of the land into the sea carried me both physically and mentally beyond the confines of my past experience. It thrust me into another world.

MICHAEL WHITT

Maintop Bay on a calm day

7-30 I met Chuck, who taught biology at Bowdoin College in Maine, and his two sons, George and Bill, for the drive to Drake Bay. We arrived at the fish dock at 6:15 A.M.; it was dead calm and overcast. I rowed out for *Angelina* and brought her up to the dock, took on fuel and loaded the passengers. We cleared Chimney Rock at 7:20 A.M. The ocean was a succession of gentle swells that pitched the boat pleasantly. We saw guillemots, murres and a few sooty shearwaters, but no mammals.

It was so calm that we circumnavigated the South Farallones. We toured Breaker (Maintop) Bay. As the name implies, this body of water, which opens into the prevailing winds, is usually rough and veiled in mist from the constant pouring of heavy seas into it. After several passes through the bay, rarely entered except by abalone divers, we went around West End to view Great Arch Rock which, also being on the weather side of the island, many visitors never see. Rounding Indian Head, where many auklets were feeding, we could see the two houses situated at the inland extremity of the marine terrace that occupies the southeast part of the island. We passed between Seal Rock which, true to its name, hosted many Steller sea lions, and Mussel Flat. Coasting by East Landing, we lingered at the mouth of Great Murre Cave, in and out of which murres circulated like bees in and out of a hive. The calm had allowed us a close passage around the rugged shoreline of South Farallones.

We dropped anchor in Fisherman Bay, and Dave came out in the raft to help us land. I took one of the boys and we rowed in to Angelina Beach. Steve Morrell was there to help us drag the shore boat up on the rocks. Dave and his passengers went into North Landing.

We walked around on the old railbed of the mule-drawn car that brought the lighthouse keeper's stores from North Landing to his dwelling. After dropping off the packs we went to look at elephant seals, of which there were only two, a weaner and a young bull. Then I left the others and went to the cormorant blind.

The chicks were as large as the adults and almost ready to fledge. The way cormorants feed the young is little short of amazing. The adult, returning from a feeding foray, often lands far from the nest. There it preens and rests before beginning to advance slowly toward its young with its "armless" shuffle. When chicks spot an adult, they rush madly toward it. If the adult does not recognize a

MICHAEL WHITT

Great Arch Rock

chick as its own, it drives the chick off with its beak. The adult may retreat as its chick approaches. When the chick finally catches up with the adult, the old and young birds fence with their beaks, until the adult decides the chick belongs to it and opens its mouth. A chick then punches its head down into the throat of the adult to meet the regurgitated meal on its way up. The beak of the chick can be seen distending the neck of the adult as it gobbles its meal.

Adults often choose a precipice on which to be cornered by the young, which beat their wings energetically while they feed in the adult's esophagus. They do this for balance and to propel them down the adult's throat, as well as from excitement, like handclapping or waving in humans. Once, an adult backed from the precipice and took wing, and the two fledglings followed. They had fledged before they knew it.

BOB JONES

Southeast Farallon

The cormorant serial had come to a close. From the old-worldlike formality of the courtship and the comic venality of nest material theft, to the vicious fights that would do carnivores proud and the grotesque feeding practices, the Brandt's cormorant has an extraordinary breeding biology.

At the murre blind, I watched a pelagic cormorant feed its only nestling. This species is the most attractive of the cormorants. It is slighter than the Brandt's and double-crested species and has a beautiful green, iridescent sheen to its black plumage, a small, red gular pouch, and white nuptial patches on the flanks. It nests solitarily or in small, dispersed groups on cliff ledges.

One adult pelagic relieved another at the nest. The incoming bird stood on a rock above the nest and, just out of reach of the nestling, preened and relaxed for a half hour before heeding the chick's fretting and neck-waving. It then hopped into the nest and fenced with the chick before feeding it. Why did it wait? To begin the process of digestion? To rest? To prepare the nestling for fledging by focusing its attention on the adult? Whatever its inner promptings, the instant gratification of its chick's appetite was not among them. The understanding of these strategies might be helpful to a human behaviorist. How animals and birds raise their young could provide some answers for human parents, many of whom take parenthood for granted. In child rearing, substitutes for instinct, such as intelligence and love, are not as consistent. If birds can't afford a family – not enough food – and if they know in time, they don't lay eggs.

They aren't too busy making money, pursuing careers, going to meetings, arguing, partying and travelling to raise their young to be successful breeders of future generations of the species. A comparison of seabird chick mortality with casualty rates of accident, homicide, psychiatric illness, drug abuse and alcoholism among the youth of so-called advanced countries would be enlightening. Seabird chicks die from starvation; human children suffer from parental indifference. Our brain may be superior, but it requires more than food, water and perfunctory proclamations of love to develop: it needs attention and real love.

A female Brandt's cormorant went up to a nest in which there appeared to be a dead nestling. The adult poked the nestling with its beak, and the young bird yawned and hopped away. Could the parent have been turning it out? Could it have been saying, in effect: OK, let's get off your duff and start fledging? Later, a pelagic cormorant came and perched nearby. The young Brandt's uttered a small gutteral sound and began frantically waving its beak in the direction of the adult pelagic, which ignored it.

The puffin or sea parrot with the unhatched egg came and stood outside its tunnel. The puffin is that curious blend of the ridiculous and sublime that so often occurs in nature. It is droll, imperious, secretive and transparent all at the same time. Its beak does not appear to have developed solely in response to specialized feeding habits; it is also an ornament for mating purposes and a source of delight to humans. It can also deliver a painful bite to fingers.

The murres had fledged and only a few adults remained scattered on the cliffs.

On the way down, I found an auklet sitting on a recently hatched nestling. It was not until 1968 here on the Farallones that two biologists, Speich and Manuwal, discovered that Cassin's auklets have a gular pouch for holding food for the young. As the foraging adult cannot reach its burrow until nightfall without danger of gull predation, it must provide in one meal – two meals when the nestling can be left alone – sufficient nourishment for the chick. The logic of this adaption is manifest in retrospect, yet the presence of the gular pouch went undetected until recently.

I retrieved two guillemot nestlings that were half-feathered and half-downy. Their legs were dark and their mouth linings were pale orange; both would turn bright red in the adult stage. The nestlings made barely audible squeaking sounds.

Gull chicks were wandering over a large area. Marked like hyenas, they fit the ugly duckling model very well. Though unattractive, their appearance provides excellent camouflage, which appears unnecessary here, as they have no predators now that the ravens are gone. Impeccably dressed adults dived and strafed me with guano. Western gulls are similar to some *Homo sapiens* – so meticulous in their hygiene and dress – whose behavior is in marked contrast to their appearance.

I watched the Coast Guard chief put off the island a man and woman who had landed from a sailboat tied up to the East Landing buoy. Before PRBO arrived on the scene, such visits were accommodated by the Coast Guard. To protect the nesting birds from disturbance and gull predation and to protect the habitat – a casual stroll off the path would crush many auklet burrows and, during breeding season, their inhabitants – no uninvited visitors are now allowed on the island.

It was the calmest day at the Farallones that I could remember, but if the weather is true to form, tomorrow will be rough.

Dodging me, a low flying guillemot dropped a small octopus at my feet. I also saw guillemots bringing sculpins to their young.

A young gull about to fledge stood on the edge of a precipice, flapping its wings and hopping up and down. A gust of wind at the right time would have gotten it airborne. As it was, it turned and walked back from the edge before that happened. It repeated this exercise many times without taking off.

On the way back to the house, I encountered Ainley weighing ashy storm-petrel chicks. One chick, a black drop of down, weighed 10 grams, another 17.

Common murre

Some adults were still on eggs; one burrow had a hatchling lying in the remnants of its shell. Then I ran into Steve Morrell,who was looking at sea parrots on Seal Rock through the spotting scope.

That night, gathered around the kitchen table, we made journal entries for the day, and Chuck talked about the studies that were in progress on Kent Island. After looking at Dave's book on Atlantic puffins, I went to bed. The others got up at 2:00 A.M. to net petrels, but I didn't go. The wind came up and they got only three.

7-31 When I awoke it was blowing, the windows rattling in their frames. Looking through the lichen-encrusted glass, I saw white water everywhere. I dressed and went over to check on *Angelina* and to see whether we could launch the shoreboat. The water was churning in Breaker Bay. I could hear the barking of the sea lions mingled with the roar of the surf. The wind made walking an effort.

Fisherman Bay was foamy from breaking surf, but I thought we could launch the boat without too much difficulty; Chuck needed to return today.

I hurried back and prepared breakfast. I awakened the Huntingtons and Dave, and we ate quickly, packed and headed for North Landing. Dave took Chuck and the gear out in the rubber raft, and I rowed the boys out from Angelina Beach. We departed the Farallones at 8:30 A.M. and picked up the buoy at Drake Bay at 12:30 P.M., the trip taking about an hour longer than

Angelina in Fisherman Bay *by Frederick J. Watson*

usual due to heavy head seas and the necessity of throttling back to reduce pounding. We still took spray over the cabin all the way.

We passed a Navy ship and encountered a small, roving band of Dall porpoises in their usual locus midway between the mainland and the Farallones. The fog withdrew as we approached the coast and it was quite beautiful, the wind having cleansed the air, brightening the white cliffs that rose behind the gleaming waters of Drake Bay.

After I discharged the Huntingtons at the dock, tied *Angelina* to her mooring and rowed ashore, we drove up to the lighthouse quarters, where we met the Coast Guard chief, Gerald Anderson, who took us down to the light. To get a better view of the murre colony, we climbed down to a ledge only a few hundred feet above the water where there was a rusty boiler, all that was left of an old foghorn. The red algae was thick and luxuriant on the cliff face. A lovely garden of seaside daisy, lizard tail, poppy, goldfields, cat's ear, buckwheat, yarrow and phacelia grew on narrow shelves of the cliff, where a thin layer of soil clung. Just below us, the murres circulated to and from their rock, and the gutteral sounds of the colony blew up to us on the wind.

8-3 I drove out to Drake Bay to pump out *Angelina*. Crossing Inverness Ridge with its dark cloak of bishop pine, I traveled through the alder bottom, dense with willow and salmonberry, before coming to the short causeway at the head of Schooner Bay, one of the branches of Drake Estero. To the right is a pickleweed marsh with a network of sloughs frequented by cinnamon teal during migration. Entering an expanse of dune dotted with yellow lupine, I could see to the left another branch of Drake Estero, Creamery Bay, where milk and butter were shipped by boat to San Francisco in the old days. Rising to higher ground, I had my first view out to sea; here you get a good idea whether it is going to be calm, rough or too rough to go out. Passing the Ocean View Ranch above Barries Bay, I saw the shore curve south toward Double Point. The ranches, protected by ragged lines of Monterey cypress disheveled by the wind, are nestled into hollows or folds of the peninsular landscape. Holstein cattle grazed the green hills, and black-tailed deer were scattered about in small groups. I often had to stop at one of the ranches to let a dairy herd cross, and I had tarried before at the A Ranch to watch the birth of a calf. Leaving shore is always like birth for me: I feel the invisible umbilicus attaching me to the solid and dependable ground underfoot snap with the first sea-heave, setting me adrift in a new and unpredictable realm.

The road twists over the peninsula – which itself rises and falls like a set of standing waves – trending upward toward the headlands, which crest dramatically and then drop abruptly into the sea. At the base of the headlands, the one-lane road down to the fish docks takes off, skirting a rocky outcrop before descending to Drake Bay. A hill across the way is stair-stepped by cow trails. On calm days like today, the flat surface of the bay is rippled by a succession of small waves forming concentrically around its perimeter. The white cliffs, seen at an angle, were dull in the overcast. The fishing fleet was gathered near the docks.

A lenticular opening between Inverness Ridge to the east and the low ceiling revealed the sunrise for a short while, first as a rich roseate smear and then as a blinding reflection of the sun on the water as if the sun were rising out of the bay. Later, rays of the sun, obscured by dense overcast, slanted through narrow openings in the clouds and fell with momentary splendor on the leaden waters. Then the sun was once more quenched by the clouds, the day again dominated by hues of gray, and the sky fitted snuggly over the earth like a lid. With low overcast there is a certain intimacy, a closeness that is lacking on clear days.

On my return to Inverness, two spiker bucks jumped across the road in front of me.

F.J. Watson

VI

Landbird Wave

Who knows but every bird that cuts the airy way
is an immense world of delight closed to the senses
five.

Blake

*D*uring the spring and autumn migrations, when weather conditions are right, many species of terrestrial birds make a landfall at the Farallones. Fog and low overcast, which prevent the birds from using the sun and stars for orientation and from seeing land at a distance, account for the birds' navigational error. Fortunately, they are able to make a rest stop at the Farallones. Most landbirds visiting the islands spend either all or part of the year in California, or migrate from northern breeding grounds to the tropics over the Pacific flyway. Present also are a number of vagrants, i.e. birds that are far from their usual migration routes. Dr. Dave DeSante has postulated that these birds are probably victims of right-left disorientation, which sends them from their northeastern nesting sites down the Pacific coast, rather than down the Atlantic flyway. Another possible explanation is that these birds are members of more recently evolved species undergoing "adaptive radiation," meaning that vagrants might be pathfinders in search of new habitat. In any event, the birds are way off their usual course.

Five species of terrestrial birds have been known to breed on Southeast Farallon: peregrine falcon, burrowing owl, common raven, rock wren and house finch. Not included are California quail, which was introduced, and house sparrow and starling, which are non-native. Now only the rock wren breeds sporadically.

On October 2,1972, Jim Lewis estimated that 10,000 landbirds were on Southeast Farallon. Lewis, who was on the island with only one volunteer, called John Smail, director of PRBO, and asked him for additional personnel to help census and band the wayward birds. John in turn asked if I could take Bill Clow, Art Earle, Steve Long and Jack Guggolz to the Farallones. I eagerly acceded to his request and moved *Angelina* to the Rod and Boat Club in Bolinas to prepare for an early departure the following day.

10-4-72 Weather was foggy and wind calm when we cast off. Bumping over the surf on the bar, we made for the buoy that marks Duxbury Reef. Soon the mainland receded from view and, well supplied with expert birders scanning the horizon for seabirds, *Angelina* rode easily over the big swell. The direction finder was not working, and being without an automatic pilot, I took a box compass and moved to the gaff well to watch birds as I steered. We saw pink-footed and sooty shearwaters, pomarine and parasitic jaegers, a rhinoceros auklet, many Cassin's auklets, and northern and red phalaropes. Also seen were a hoary bat and a gray whale – these two being at the extremes of mass in the mammal kingdom – one the size of a small bird weighing a few grams and the other 40 feet long and 30 tons.

After we had been underway for the prescribed length of time and had not sighted land, I shut down the engine to listen for the foghorn at Southeast Farallon and the sound of surf breaking on the island. Hearing neither, I sent Art Earle forward to look for white water, and we again got underway. Soon Art cried out that white water was dead ahead. We were just off Middle Farallon, called "the pimple" by fishermen. It is a single rock that was almost awash in the heavy swell. Watching birds had gotten me slightly off course; if we had missed Middle Farallon, our next landfall was Hawaii!

Visibility was less than a mile, and the South Farallones were shrouded in fog three miles to the southeast. Soon the islands began to emerge from the gray loom of fog, their ghostly castellations ringed at the base by a bright white line of surf. We came up to the buoy off East Landing where Jim and Bruce Webb were waiting for us. The heavy swell breaking around the island made getting ashore problematic. A visitor in 1874 wrote that "the fury of the waves makes landing at all times difficult, and for the most part impossible," words that well described our predicament. But the report of 10,000 landbirds on the island stimulated our determination and ingenuity.

On calm days the boat is brought under the Billy Pugh, a cone-shaped rope net with a floor, and people and stores are transferred directly to the island. At

DAVID AINLEY

Middle Farallon

other times, the boat is tied to the buoy and the island's Boston whaler is low-ered to serve as a go-between from boat to net. On days like today, landing is usually not attempted.

Communicating over the roar of surf by yells and gestures, we decided to lower the whaler and land our passengers directly onto the rocks. The motor of the whaler was started just before it hit the water, as any delay might have allowed the boat to be carried on the rocks by the surf. As the whaler motored out to *Angelina*, Jim moved from the landing out to a point of rock (now called Water Temp. Point because water temperature was measured here) around which the surf broke from two directions, thus dampening somewhat its height and force.

Billy, Art, Jack and I climbed into the outboard boat. Running the whaler, I let the surf carry the bow upon the rock where Lewis waited, and the man in front handed over his pack. We sagged back in the trough and circled out of danger. Choosing another wave and riding up on it, we landed the pack's owner, who grasped Lewis's hand and was pulled ashore. We repeated this exer-cise until Bill, Art and Jack were safely on the island. The whaler was then snatched up with the hoist, its motor running, and Steve and I took *Angelina* to Fisherman Bay and anchored. As I recall, we had not landed here as in the past to avoid disturbing the sea lions. But it was too rough to leave *Angelina* at the buoy at East Landing.

After finding beds and stowing our packs, we headed for the Farallon forest, which consists of two small Monterey cypresses next to the Coast Guard quar-ters and a low Monterey pine surrounded by a Helgoland trap, which had an opening near the ground leading by a narrow passage to a large cage. It was used for trapping ground birds. Mist nets thrown up near the cypresses caught birds on the wing to and from the trees. Birds collected were weighed, sexed, banded and released. Age, whether immature or adult, was noted and nutritional status determined by estimating fat stores through the transparent skin.

The day of our arrival 60 species of landbirds numbering 3,407 individuals were counted. Among them were merlin, short-eared owl, yellow-shafted flicker, sage thrasher, Townsend's solitaire, evening grosbeak and Lapland longspur. There were four vagrant warblers: magnolia, blackpoll, palm and ovenbird. Vaux's swifts and violet-green swallows circulated around the lighthouse along with western gulls. Including seabirds, ducks and shore birds, 95 species were logged. Bill Clow, who made the entries in the journal that night as we sat around the kitchen table, summed it up well: "What a beautiful trip from Bolinas to an island covered with birds!"

10-5 Clear. Light to gentle breezes caressed the island. Over half the landbirds departed with the improved visibility. One hundred and sixty-one birds were banded today. Uncommon to extremely rare visitants seen were: least and Hammond's flycatchers; yellow-shafted flicker; sage thrasher; Virginia's warbler; Cassin's finch; green-tailed towhee; Clark's nutcracker; Tennessee warbler; American redstart; rose-breasted grosbeak; and clay-colored, white-throated and tree sparrows.The Clark's nutcracker was an island record. Clow, who had eagerly assumed the duties of journalist, wrote at the end of another memorable day: "Numbers much diminished. Everyone frantically running around with birds."

10-6 Clear. A gentle breeze blew. The number of landbirds was halved again. One Baird's and seven pectoral sandpipers were seen today, both species nesting on the tundra inside the Arctic circle and wintering in South America. Elliott Coues, an Army surgeon and founder of the American Ornithologists' Union, named the former for Spencer Baird, Secretary of the Smithsonian Institution. A friend of Audubon's, Baird was the most important ornithologist of his time "in all that related to the technicalities of the science," to quote Coues.

A blue grosbeak was netted and banded. An adult male the color of lapis lazuli, its brilliant plumage fairly glowed in the hand.

Six hundred brown pelicans were counted.

What makes landbirding on Southeast Farallon special is not only the variety, the large numbers in a small space, and the likelihood of rare birds, but the absence of cover – plus the opportunity to handle the birds.

Always a good host, Jim Lewis prepared an excellent meal of mussels picked at low tide. Clow wrote in the journal: "Several monarch butterflies were observed as well as one 'skipper' type butterfly and one 'sulfur' type butterfly. One grasshopper was seen by Jack Guggolz. East winds (which were not reflected in the weather data) brought much smog and haze and maybe had something to do with the butterflies' arrival. Who knows? Large numbers of meadowlarks were still seen; however a few (10) were noticeably weak and two were picked up and, WOW, what a beautiful bird to have in hand!!"

Also recorded was this observation on the formerly ubiquitous kelp fly, an often unappreciated endemic species: "Ah! The wonderfulness of a bird wave: no flies. NO FLIES!"

10-7 The weather remained clear with a wind force of 10 knots. Only autumn brings these lovely days without wind or fog.

Jim wanted to go to the North Farallones, so he and I trolled up and back. We didn't catch any salmon, but we did catch a "mess" of yellow-tailed rockfish. Jack and I cleaned them at North Landing, and Jim cooked them for dinner.

Only 278 landbirds were counted today; the number of species was down from 60 to 39. A little pied-billed grebe was seen offshore. A Clark's nutcracker was again seen, probably the same bird as before. Strange to see this denizen of the high Sierra frequenting the Farallones, with its puny forest of three trees.

Thirteen hundred and fifty pelicans, mostly adults, were on and around the island. A hoary bat flitted about. An elephant seal with deep gashes from a shark bite hauled out.

A curious silence prevailed, with the gulls reduced in number and less vocal, the murres and guillemots absent, and the wind and seas calm. The quiet gave us a chance to hear the landbirds: Clow had found the longspur among all the sparrows by hearing its call.

10-8 Dead calm with broken clouds. I got off late, after having taken a last tour of the island to look for rare birds that might have come in overnight and then having to clean *Angelina's* starter before the motor would turn over. I returned alone, arriving at the Golden Gate in the late afternoon. Inside the span, I ran into a traffic jam of Sunday boaters. Dodging sailboats, I made my way to Richardson Bay and dropped anchor off Sausalito by the old dry dock with the word LOVE scrawled on it. After being waved off several piers by owners tired of hippy boaters – I had a long beard at the time – I landed under a large pier and dragged the boat up on the rocks. I hoped it would go unnoticed for a day or two. I got to the road just in time to see Barbara, who had given up on me, driving out of town. I was marooned in Sausalito with all the Sunday tourists – and in culture shock after five days on the Farallones – until my wife could return from Inverness and rescue me.

When Sausalito was still a fishing village, it must have been one of the most beautiful and tranquil places on San Francisco Bay. Then the insidious process of degradation that attacks most beautiful places in America, especially those in the shadow of a big city, transformed it into a tourist trap and residential community for the wealthy. First, tourists flock to any picturesque village, causing traffic congestion and higher prices. Next, real estate values start to escalate. Attracted by the money, owners sell all vacant land at increasing prices. Taxes go up. Then a bad year for the local economy – in this case, fishing – occurs. Fishermen, hard hit by the slump and in need of money, sell out. The village, now too expensive for fishermen to inhabit, is separated from its original *raison d'etre*. As population in the area increases and land values and taxes continue to rise, the village becomes non-functional, a destination for tourists and vagrants and a suburb for commuters. The village is no longer poor, but thriving. It has become a lovely nonentity.

VII

Reflections

A flight of pelicans
Is nothing lovelier to look at;
The flight of the planets is nothing nobler; all the arts
lose virtue
Against the essential reality
Of creatures going about their business among the equally
Earnest elements of nature.

Jeffers

I sold *Angelina* in 1973, when I couldn't get the leak in the shaft log sealed. We had moved from Seahaven, and I no longer had access to my mooring, so I anchored her out at Marshall Boatworks. She had to be watched closely during storms, several times shipping enough water to be in danger of sinking. After office hours, I would drive to Marshall, row out through the rain and waves and pump her out. With a good deal of sadness, I finally sold her. Our daughter Lazuli was born that year, and I thought I would replace *Angelina* with a pleasure boat more suitable for a family, but it was not to be. And besides, I could not dissociate a boat from work.

I had not been to the Farallones in two years when Dave asked me to accompany Bob Jones and him on a short trip to collect otoliths, the ear stones of fishes.

9-7-74 I picked up Dave and Harriet Huber, a PRBO biologist studying the burgeoning population of elephant seals at the Farallones, and we drove to Sausalito, where we met the other members of the party and Charlie Merrill, whose boat *Cimba* would take us to the island. Charlie is one of the founders of the Farallon Patrol, a group of Oceanic Society members who volunteer their boats to Point Reyes Bird Observatory. The light was automated in 1972, and the Coast Guard's irregular runs no longer met all of PRBO's needs. The Farallon Patrol picked up where *Angelina* left off and eventually assumed full responsibility for getting PRBO to and from the island. It has been an essential part of the Farallon program.

The presence of Harriet and Lise Thomsen, Bob Jones's wife, on an overnight outing to the islands represented a big change in policy since my last trip in 1972. Women and children were banned from the Farallones in the early 1960s, when the Coast Guard deemed their presence too expensive to support. Rumor had it that an adulterous affair involving Coast Guard personnel was also a contributing factor. When Coast Guardsmen moved off the island, women were permitted to return.

It was clear and sunny in the yacht harbor, but thick fog poured like a cataract over Wolfback Ridge, and a long, fingerlike projection of it reached through the Golden Gate and tentatively probed San Francisco Bay. As we ran out on a flood tide, we penetrated the fog's curtain and were enveloped by its gloomy wilderness of gray. The blue sky, bright slopes, flashing windows reflecting the rising sun and smooth waters of Richardson Bay yielded to the fog's blindfold and the heave and roll of the sea. A small fleet of sport boats passed us on its way to the salmon grounds. Visibility was less than one-half mile. On my first trip as a passenger, I had to fight a feeling of superfluity.

We saw many sooty shearwaters skimming the water, peeling off the surface, wheeling and laying breast to wave again and again. The silent repetitiveness of this pattern embroidered my memories of *Angelina*, as I looked out over the lumpy waters.

We heard the foghorn before we saw the island. As we got closer, the crest, guano-white and stark, emerged from the fog. The wind shifted and the foghorn became inaudible. It was calm with a light breeze as we approached East Landing. The seas were so calm that Charlie guided *Cimba* in under the Billy Pugh, which was lowered over the bow. Packs were stuffed inside and passengers stood on the outside clinging to the net, as it was hoisted onto the landing. Charlie tied *Cimba* to the buoy, and the Boston whaler picked up those still aboard.

After lunch we set out for Maintop on West End to look for otoliths. These tiny bones are secreted in the inner ear and help the fish maintain its equilibrium. Otoliths are very hard and escape digestion by a bird predator. They can be collected on a breeding ground or roosting site, identified by an expert in fishes and used to determine the bird's diet, without having disturbed the bird during feeding. The double-crested cormorant, which is the cormorant commonly seen inland, nests here in seclusion, undisturbed even by biologists, except for the banding of young before fledging. It came precariously close to extinction on the Farallon Islands during the years of egging.

In the calm, we were covered by the kelp flies, which crawled in our ears and nose and up our shirt sleeves and pant legs and got tangled in our hair and beard. Kelp flies make you long for a stiff wind or, better yet, a landbird wave. I had never seen the flies so thick. I could see a few elephant seals dozing on a sandy flat below. They appeared to be stained with tar which, on examination with field glasses, turned out to be clots of kelp flies on their coats. Their large eyes were also covered with flies. They listlessly flipped sand on their backs to cool themselves and ward off the insects.

BOB JONES

The Billy Pugh

Dead cormorant and gull chicks were strewn about the island, reflecting the high infant mortality among seabirds.

The flies were maddening, but Dave continued collecting in silence. After brushing away flies with my container and spilling my otoliths, I gave up and sought a prominence with a breeze and a view. A calm sea lapped at the island. The nesting areas were deserted. Near the water, a few unfledged cormorants were being fed, the chick stuffing its head in the mouth of the parent and beating its wings. One adult tried to peck a tardy chick from its perch to make it fledge. The breeding cycle was winding down; fledging was almost completed. The landbird wave would begin later this month or early next. Spring and summer belonged to the seabirds, fall to migrant landbirds and winter to the elephant seals. It was a busy year. Now was a brief pause in activity.

Today was like a lazy, southern summer afternoon, warm and still with droves of insects. A few pelicans roosted on offshore rocks. White heads were folded on faded gray bodies with white fringes like salt encrustations. Skimming the water in file, they were like a company of transmogrified ancients arriving from the mists of prehistory to witness the strange conditions of the present,

STEVE MORRELL

Female elephant seals quibbling

where the human population explosion was threatening the balance of the species.

Seal Rock, to the southeast, might have been called Shark Rock, as its crest is like the dorsal fin of a shark. A group of California sea lions was rafted in Fisherman Bay. Several had their front flippers crooked in the air. When seas are calm, they congregate like this.

The Farallones are granite peaks rising from the continental shelf. Along with the Point Reyes Peninsula, they are part of the Salinian block that has migrated 350 miles north along the San Andreas Fault, which runs on a line through Bodega Bay and Harbor, Tomales Bay and Bolinas Lagoon. Before San Francisco Bay formed, the Sacramento River poured through the Golden Gate and flowed past the Farallones, much as it does the Sutter Buttes today. Before the end of the last ice age, it was possible to reach the Farallones overland.

Walking back from Maintop to the Jordan Channel, we were careful not to cave in the auklet burrows riddling the ground. They made me think of the loess houses found in China. The thin layer of soil in which the burrows are dug is composed of guano and decomposed granite. Time and weather have made it possible for the auklet to live in a house excavated from excrement.

Every burrow, niche, crack and crevice is occupied by underground nesters: Cassin's and rhinoceros auklets, ashy and Leach's storm-petrels, pigeon guillemots and tufted puffins. The ledges and cliffs are crowded with common murres and sprinkled with pelagic cormorants. The sea terraces are home to the western gull, and the rocks and slopes of the hills are colonized by Brandt's and double-crested cormorants. The beaches are packed with elephant seals, and harbor seals haul out on Mussel Flat. The rocky shores and offshore rocks are lined with Steller and California sea lions. A Northern fur seal is occasionally found among the sea lions. Almost every inch of space is filled, both above or below ground.

Of the original inhabitants, only the sea otter is extinct, and it is likely to recur soon. Around the island circulate gray, humpbacked and blue whales.

Pods of killer whales and great white sharks cruise for seals and sea lions. The Gulf of the Farallones or, as the Spanish called it, *Ensenada de los Farallones*, is a profound ecosystem.

What makes this great profusion of life possibile? Why the Farallones? A system of currents circumscribes the North Pacific. The California Current, a section of the North Pacific Gyre, drops down along the coast of North America past the Farallones and swings back west at the tip of Baja California. In the spring, the prevailing northwesterlies begin to blow and the surface waters of the California Current are pushed offshore; deep, cold, nutrient-rich water upwells into the photic zone, where sunlight causes a lush plankton bloom. When the plankton multiply, the response travels through the food web to krill, squid, rockfish, birds and mammals.

What began for Dave as a study of birds on the Farallones, expanded naturally to include prey species and thence around the food web to the ocean environment. As the weather phenomenon called El Niño proved, the entire Pacific is involved in local ecology. El Niño – the Christ Child – first observed in the Humbolt Current, which in the Southern Hemisphere is analogous to our California Current, is ironically so called because it occurred around Christmas, the austral summer solstice. El Niño is caused by a reversal or cessation of the trade winds, which customarily blow from east to west, bringing a reflux of warm water from the tropics. This backflow of warm water subdues upwelling of cold, nutrient-laden water – or upwells warm, nutrient-poor water – and blights the plankton bloom. So the study now includes the Pacific Ocean from the Antarctic to the latitude of the Farallones. Dave has devised a strategy to include his two widely disparate sites of research into one project! As all the world's oceans converge around the Antarctic, the stage is set for a global radiation of what began as a local inquiry. This has come at a time when pollution and degradation of the world's environment are survival issues. Knowledge of bird and marine biology has become a critical skill in monitoring environmental health. While my profession of medicine impacts the immediate health of individuals – and in that respect is more dramatic – the protection of the oceans and the atmosphere is the ultimate public health concern.

On the other hand, a knowledge of Pacific weather patterns and their effects on the food web can explain seabird die-offs and poor fishing and relieve fears of insidious pollution of the ocean. Dave was able to explain a recent die-off of murres and their young, rhinoceros auklets and puffins along the central coast of California in just such a manner, and forestall unfounded speculations that a mysterious pollutant was the killer.

Farallon weed was unseasonably in bloom. In the late winter and early spring, before the gulls and cormorants pull it all up for their nests, *Lasthenia minor*, var. *maritima*, with its yellow flowers, transforms the "barren" gray rocks of Southeast Farallon to a subtle, lovely lime-green. Approached from the sea when the weed is in bloom, the island looks as if it were tinted by fancy, or as if a color transparency had been drawn over it.

At dusk, fog insidiously closed the island in.

9-8 The fog withdrew in the night, and I awoke early to clear skies. A moderate breeze blew, white-hatching the sea. I went looking for the blackpoll warbler I had glimpsed yesterday, but couldn't find it. With good visibility and a tail wind, it had probably departed for its winter home in South America. I looked at a nine-day-old ashy storm-petrel chick, a pile of respiring down. Another storm-petrel chick was almost ready to fledge. It was a beautiful charcoal-gray bird with shiny black beak and tube nose and bright black eye. Even with field glasses, spotting scopes and radio telemetry, a burrow-nesting seabird's life is to a great extent a mystery.

Before departing, Dave, Bob and I went to Murre Cave to look for more otoliths. A few pelagic cormorants sailed out of the cave as we entered. The walls were a dark green and the footing was slippery with guano. The cave is high-ceilinged with a hole at the top, through which fresh air circulates. Bob found a spectacular lemon-yellow nudibranch in a tidepool on the floor of the cave. Bob also found a gelatinous, fleshlike mass filled with otoliths and fish bones. We at first thought it might be a bird's stomach rejected by a gull. After finding more of these "stomachs" on subsequent trips and examining them closely, Dave concluded that they were not "stomachs" at all, but rubbery secretions by which cormorants envelop and expel indigestible material from their stomachs. Dave thinks it is also a means of expelling round worms, abundant in these castings, which are soft versions of the pellets cast by raptors.

We departed East Landing at 11 A.M. Charlie and his crewman had spent an uncomfortable night tied up to the buoy there. The boat had rolled in the swell all night, and the flies had been bad. Dave had invited them ashore, and when they declined, I had suggested they anchor in Fisherman Bay, where I had kept *Angelina*. Charlie had not wanted to do this either.

Dave and I rode all the way back on the flying bridge, and the view was grand. Dave religiously counted murres, while I took in the sights. Fog obscured Point Reyes, but Mount Wittenberg, with its crown of trees and yellow forehead of grass, was visible. The weather was also clear to the south, and we could see Point Montara and San Bruno Mountain. Mount Tamalpais's summit rose above the coastal haze, which curtained the Golden Gate. I could easily see how San Francisco Bay went undiscovered for over 200 years by Spanish mariners and English pirates. The Bay was first entered by ship in 1775, six years after it had been discovered by members of Gaspar de Portola's overland expedition. The best argument against Drake's having careened the Golden Hinde at Point San Quentin is that he made no mention of San Francisco Bay, perhaps the best harbor in the world. Even on a clear day, the Golden Gate is not visible until you are close to shore, and then the line of the East Bay hills seems to be continuous with the Marin headlands and the San Francisco Peninsula.

We saw a pomarine and a parasitic jaeger. These birds nest in the Far North, where they feed on lemmings. They winter at sea and pirate their food from other species. Sleek and rakish birds, they are wonderful fliers.

Many sooty shearwaters coursed by on stiff wings close to the water's surface.

DAVID AINLEY

Western gull

One withdrew its wing quickly to avoid wetting it. Two shearwaters landed, dipped their beaks in the water and dove. Others flew directly into the water. Dave described this as pursuit diving. Shearwaters continue to "fly" underwater like the alcids.

The boat rolled and yawed pleasantly in the quartering seas. The day was fine and sunny. Many murres and gulls were on the water. Pelicans rowed through the wind. Gradually the RCA buildings and poles on Bolinas Mesa came into view, and the monstrous Sutro Tower materialized above San Francisco. The seas were choppy in the Potato Patch or, as it is officially known, the Four Fathom Bank. In the Golden Gate, the water danced and whirled to the music of the wind and currents. We entered the haven of the Bay, passing through the cold shadow of the span lying on the bright green water.

In the Sausalito Yacht Harbor, owners of large motor launches and sailboats sat on deck sunning themselves, drinking highballs and reading the Sunday paper. I preferred to come home to Drake Bay, where the only sounds are the scoters' soft whistle and occasionally the crazy laugh of a loon, and the only craft, the salmon boat. But the trip had been great, and I enjoyed the change from being down in the house of *Angelina* to being up on the flying bridge of a Grand Banks trawler.

We glided into Charlie's slip and made fast the lines.

Sausalito was jammed with people and cars. As we drove out, I recalled the time when we had arrived in Drake Bay to find a sailboat anchored among the fishing fleet. The evening had been beautiful and calm, with columns of sunlight pouring through the clouds and forming pools of light on the lead-gray water. Having been obscured by cloud, the sun had suddenly reappeared on the horizon just before it set: a huge, discrete, red disk.

As we were leaving, after cleaning some ling cod we had caught at Stormy Stack, near Double Point, the two men from the sailboat had scrambled up on the dock and hailed us. Tanned and stylishly dressed in yachting attire, they had asked without a word of greeting if there was a taxi service! We had laughed and said there wasn't any. They had then asked how far it was to a popular French restaurant in Point Reyes Station. Twenty-five miles. Having sailed up from Sausalito just to eat there, they had wanted to know if we could give them a ride in. We had said OK, but warned them it might be difficult hitching a ride back, as there were few cars at night. Were we sure there was no taxi in Point Reyes? We were sure.

As we drove up the hill from the dock, we saw them rowing out to their boat. Had it not been for the establishment of Point Reyes National Seashore they might well have been able to call a taxi, or perhaps even to have found a seafood restaurant at dockside.

* * * *

Another two-and-a-half years passed before I returned to the Farallones. Bob Fisher, the local veterinarian, and I went out with Charlie Hendrickson of the Farallon Patrol. Bob assisted PRBO with its marine mammal research, and I provided medical consultation, often by radio telephone, with island personnel and performed physical examinations for Antarctic researchers. Charlie and I had met over a heating problem at my Point Reyes Station office.

4-23 We left the Clipper Yacht Harbor in Sausalito early in the morning aboard Charlie's sailboat *Calypso*. It was low overcast, and we had to motor for lack of wind. I was coming down with another case of islomania and looked forward to a few days on Southeast Farallon, surrounded by the ocean. I was also afflicted with seasickness and nearly heaved; Charlie opined that a man in my condition would give a million dollars for a square foot of land. I really couldn't agree with that, but I didn't argue with the skipper.

Seasickness is a curious malady. When I skippered *Angelina*, I got seasick only once. When I go out as a passenger, I am more likely to get seasick than not. Overstimulation of the inner ear or labyrinth and an unstable horizon are thought to account for the condition, but level of involvement on the boat, emotions and fatigue must also be important factors. The one time I got seasick on *Angelina*, I had been up all night attending a home birth. As the morning was beautiful, and I was high from shepherding a new life into the world, I decided to return the boat from Drake to Tomales Bay for repairs. As I turned the corner below the lighthouse on Point Reyes, I ran into dense fog. At about the same time, I saw a small flock of what I thought were rhinoceros auklets. They were enough of a novelty at the time for me to want a closer look to be sure of my identification and to watch them at close range. Visibility was very poor, and the land had dissolved in fog. I circled around and around chasing the little creatures, until I was satisfied on both counts. When I resumed my compass course, I did not know quite where I was.

If anything, the visibility became poorer as I motored north; it got down to less than 100 feet. After I had been out long enough to reach Tomales Point, I realized that my chances of finding the whistle buoy that marked it and the way into Tomales Bay were poor-to-none. I cut the motor to listen for the whistle. Not hearing it, I began to get seasick. I lay down on the deck and tried to feel better, so I could plan my next move. As I wasn't very familiar with Bodega Bay and its coastline and didn't want to miss Bodega Head, which would have put me out to sea, I decided to proceed very slowly due east, until I made a landfall that I hoped I would recognize. As soon as I made my decision, the seasickness resolved as quickly as it had come. I had only to be careful that *Angelina* not get caught in the surf and capsize. Soon I began to feel the heave of the ground swell, and in a moment I saw white water. A large rock slowly emerged from the fog: Elephant Rock at McClure's Beach. I moved offshore to avoid foul ground, skirted Bird Rock and, unable to cross the breaking bar at the entrance to Tomales Bay, made my way to the safety of Bodega Harbor. I concluded, on the basis of my unplanned experiment, that fatigue and fear were also strong determinants of seasickness, and a high level of involvement in the operation of the boat was a good antidote.

Immature western gull

Approaching Southeast Farallon we saw two puffins on the water. Several gray whales spouted off East Landing. We kept missing the buoy, until Ron LeValley, a PRBO biologist, coming out for us in the Boston whaler, took the line and passed it through the eye-ring. Ron then took us to the Billy Pugh, positioned low over the water, and we were lifted onto the island. *Calypso* returned to the mainland.

The origin of the name Billy Pugh piqued my curiosity, but I couldn't track it down. None of the old salts I asked had ever heard of it. I recalled Blind Pew in *Treasure Island* and wondered if Billy Pugh was also from the romantic past. Finally, Dave suggested that I ask Pete White, a PRBO volunteer, who is interested in the history of the Farallones. Pete recalled that the net was manufactured in Texas. Calling "Information," he found a Billy Pugh Company in Corpus Christi, where I had gone to high school. Slowly, from underneath layers of more recent memory, my connection with this name began to emerge. My first real job had been scraping barnacles from boat bottoms for the Billy Pugh

Steller sea lions – large bull on right

Boatworks! I called Billy recently and he confirmed what I remembered. He manufactures the nets that go by his name; he also designed and manufactured the nets that were used to recover NASA astronauts from their capsule after its splashdown.

I took Bob on a tour of the island, with the exception of West End, which was off-limits. At the cormorant blind, we saw only a few occupied nests and little activity. At North Landing we crawled to the edge of the concrete to observe without scaring a big pile of barking and shoving California sea lions.

Fisherman Bay, so called because salmon fishermen anchor there, is a place of great beauty and relative tranquility in the summertime. Sugarloaf, Arch and Aulon Rocks provide protection from the prevailing northwesterlies. The southeastern lip of the cove (Tower Point) is very shallow, and big seas from winter storms can curl into the bay, though I had anchored there without mishap in all seasons. Once during a southerly blow I had contemplated moving *Angelina* into Breaker Bay, but I was afraid that the wind would suddenly turn around to the northwest, that I could not get out to her and that she would capsize. I missed her at her familiar anchorage. Without her, I could no longer come and go freely, nor be of service to PRBO.

At the murre blind on Shubrick Point, we watched several cormorant fights. Like politicians, their polite behavior is in humorous contrast to their contrariness and venality. A bird landed at the nest site with its neck bowed. It slowly extended its neck to reveal its bright-blue gular pouch. It repeated this formal gesture as it hopped into the nest. Its mate responded in kind.

A few murres preened, and a pair of puffins loitered below the blind.

According to Dave, these two birds, identifiable by holes and nicks in their toe webs, had resided here since 1972. Puffin is the diminutive of the English word puff, and the name reflects the affection the bird inspires.

Gray whales surfaced off Shubrick Point, their numbers much increased since my earlier visits. Like elephant seals, they were nearly exterminated by commercial harvesting. These behemoths, never having escaped fully their tellurian past, remain confined to coastal waters, which made them an easy mark for whalers. With prohibitions against whaling, they have rebounded from the ultimate oblivion of extinction to resume their rightful place in the coastal community.

Bob and I had been assigned the task of reading the tags on the elephant seals at Sand Flat. The young and females are such mournful creatures, with their big watering eyes and runny noses. They were molting, their brown hair falling off and revealing their new gray coats.

Back at the house, a PRBO volunteer came in with a beautiful male lazuli bunting in turquoise breeding plumage, which shone like a gemstone in the hand.

4-24 Walked up on Lighthouse Hill. A few red maids were in bloom along the path. Sea pigeons were out on the rocks wailing, natty with red mouth and feet, black plumage and white wing patch.

With the glasses we could see a stately flotilla of eared grebes in breeding plumage like little boats all decked out for the blessing of the fleet.

Murres, sleek of head, exquisite of feather line and bright of mouth, were everywhere this morning. Like its cousin the guillemot, the murre walks on the tarsi, the fused bones of the foot, and like other diving seabirds, its feet are placed far back on its body as an aid to diving (ruddering, in its case). The use of the legs for walking is incidental, an afterthought. A few murres were mating, after bowing to one another like Orientals. Actually, I suspect it's the other way around: conventions of human behavior were copied from seabirds.

A graphic example of bird persuasion took place at a cormorant nest. A male was sitting on the nest, the female beside him, stroking and nibbling his neck. Twice she flew off and returned with a beak full of Farallon weed. She obviously wanted his attention. When she returned the second time, he stood to greet her, extending his neck and flashing his blue gular pouch. She maneuvered onto the nest, he hopped on her back and they copulated.

With one of the biologists, we fished an incubating auklet from its burrow. It stared unflinchingly at us with its opalescent eye. When we returned it to the mouth of its burrow, it scurried in on its tarsi. The puffin, an exception among the alcids, walks on its toes like other birds.

It was clear and calm at dawn, and then, the wind shifting to the east, the island was enveloped in a luminous veil of fog, which gradually withdrew leaving a hazy-bright calm. A dazzling ring of white surf divided the gray-green isle from the blue sea.

At Sea Lion Cove we watched Steller sea lions lumber out of the sea and over the rocks. A sea lion moving on land reminded me of a crutch walker the way it laboriously hitched first one side and then the other slowly forward as it lurched along. Unlike whales, pinnipeds had not been able to completely sever their attachment to land, but were compelled to return to it, even though they had lost their grace and agility walking. I thought of my son Garrett, who has cerebral palsy and walks only with assistance and great difficulty. He too is still tethered to the land, but like pinnipeds in the sea, his opportunity is in another medium. In the realm of ideas and imagination, he might roll and porpoise, arch and dive, in a way the physically fit rarely can. His bond with the earth broken, he is free to enter fully the world of mind and spirit.

A Steller cow stood watch over her dead pup. It must have been a stillbirth, as the umbilical cord with placenta was still attached. Gulls stood by waiting for the mother to abandon it. When a gull got too close, the mother lunged and drove it back. "The gulls are smart; they know it's dead," Bob said, "but the mother doesn't know yet." Maternal instinct has an inertia that makes it resist mere fact.

These sea lions were first described by Georg Steller, a German naturalist accompanying Vitus Bering when he discovered Alaska in 1741. The names of mammals and birds are evocative not only of obscure naturalists, but of far-off places and distant times. As history connects us to the past, seabirds and marine mammals relate us to remote settings. Dave tells me that recently nomenclaturists have changed the common name from Steller to northern sea lion, which serves no good purpose and nullifies the drama inherent in the current name.

In the same vein, William Healy Dall, who first described the porpoise bearing his name from specimens collected in Alaska in 1873, connects us to our own early history in the Far North. Dall went to Alaska at age 19, when he accompanied the Western Union Telegraph Expedition that was surveying a route for a telegraph cable from the United States through Canada and Alaska, across Bering Strait and Siberia to Europe! The expedition was called off when a trans-Atlantic cable was successfully laid, but Dall stayed in Alaska, becoming an authority on its wildlife and other natural resources. Our latitude is the southernmost limit of the Dall porpoise's range, but a sighting of that splendid mammal calls to mind Dall, the Far North and heroic enterprises. Someday the homogenizers will no doubt propose renaming this mammal the northern porpoise!

I went over *Farallon Journal* entries from my previous trips. The number of PRBO personnel had steadily increased since my first visit, when Dave and I were the only two bird people on the island. Prior to that, Henry Robert and Jim Lewis often spent long periods alone on the island. There were now eight volunteers, including three women, in addition to the two biologists, Ron LeValley and Steve Morrell. The research program designed by Dave was in full swing and more observers were required to gather data. The island seemed almost crowded!

Spring migrants netted today were: orange-crowned, Nashville and Audubon's warblers. I saw a yellow warbler out the window as I was looking through *The Farallon Journal*.

STEVE MORRELL

Female Steller sea lion

Sand spurry was in bloom along with Farallon weed, which had not yet all been picked by the gulls and cormorants. A bush mallow was in garish purple flower.

4-25 Early morning fog cleared. South wind was three knots.

Rafts of California sea lions were off the island, some lying in typical fashion with one front flipper extended in the air. It was warm and sunny. Bob proposed that *Zalophus* assumed this position for the same reasons that a dog lies on its back with its feet in the air, simply because it feels good.

Gulls swirled noisily above the island. They circle looking for an opportunity to raid. Any kind of disturbance is destructive, but airplanes and helicopters are the worst. The presence of such a large object in the sky, and the loud noise accompanying it, flushes all the birds within sight and hearing of the monster and provides an instant banquet for the gulls. A cormorant or murre colony's young can be wiped out.

As the eggers knew, the murre can respond to the loss of an egg by producing another, as can the cormorants. What the eggers didn't know is that murres can only respond once. Chicks are not replaced, unless it is a year of abundant food supply. Clutch size is regulated by food availability. In very lean years, no eggs are laid. This breeding economy, a measure of the birds' environmental sensitivity, is, of course, lacking for the most part in humans.

We watched a gull pluck an adult auklet from its burrow and gulp it down.

The weather was warm and sunny today. The cormorants were panting and fluttering their gular pouches. Cormorants don't have external nares and must breathe through their mouths. The elephant seals had all moved into the water to cool off. The resonant bellowing of the bulls sounded to the top of Lighthouse Hill. I watched a pair of gulls copulate. After finishing, the male declined to dismount. Instead he remained standing on the female's back. She finally walked off, and he rode five or six steps before dropping to the ground.

Wandering tattlers, olive-brown birds with smooth plumage like gabardine, hunted singly in the teeth of the surf. Gray whales spouted off Indian Head. The breast of the sea rose and fell slowly like that of a sleeping giant.

The surge channels in Breaker Bay and West End are choked with driftwood. These sea-worn timbers would make great totems if carved with animals of the Farallones and placed before the houses as they are at Alert Bay, B.C. Lying in state in the surge channels, they are monuments to the diminishing forests that produced them and the restless power of the ocean that brought them here.

4-26 Another calm day. As the sun went down, fishing boats began to gather at the island for the night. Coast Guard cutter *Point Heyer* lay at the East Landing buoy. Ron and I took some beer to trade for salmon with the fishermen and were lowered in the Boston whaler. We stopped at the cutter to drop off mail, and the crewmen grew excited when they saw the beer, the sight of it doing for them what the sight of rare birds did for us.

We motored around Shubrick Point to Fisherman Bay, where several salmon boats were anchored. The dark brimming water was full of California sea lions, drifting in large rafts. As we passed they came alive, poking their heads out of the water and craning their necks, then barking and diving. As the sea scored and worked the edges of the island, the gull cries and sea lion barking etched my memory.

We came alongside a boat from Albion. The crew were cleaning salmon. Their haul that day was worth $280, they told us. We traded two six-packs and two dollars for a large fish, which they cut in two for us. We went back to East Landing and hooked the boat up to the hoist, which lifted us out of the sea and swung us onto the cement pad. I always found it exciting, rising slowly from the water, as if I were levitating, and gazing at the panorama unfolding below me.

As dusk deepened, more fishing boats homed in on Southeast Farallon. A fine second quarter moon was high in the west. Sirius followed his master Orion, who trooped low on the horizon, and Leo, crouched above and behind, watched them pass. The Great Bear walked in the East, its luster dimmed by the lights of the Bay Area. Saturn was visible and the doves of the Pleiades fluttered faintly in the wake of the sun. Corvus flew beneath Spica, which marked the sheaf of wheat in the hand of Virgo, the goddess of justice, whose reign is yet to be fully extended to the earth and her other children.

A lovely sight: the fishing boats, their anchor lights swaying, gathering around the island for the night. The picture was all the lovelier for its rarity, the wind usually being fresh and the seas heavy.

At midnight I climbed back up Lighthouse Hill for another look. The gulls were wheeling slowly in the rotating beam of light. They flashed a bright white as the light picked them out of the darkness. Above, the stars glittered, and below, the anchor lights of the fishing fleet swayed gently. The buoy at Noonday Rock near the North Farallones blinked in the black hole of the Pacific Ocean. Scorpio was rising in the east above the garish glow of the Bay Area, the only reminder that the Farallon Islands were part of the city and county of San Francisco. St. Francis of Assisi, the namesake of this glowing city to the east, had begun his good works after hearing an image of Christ say to him, "Francis, repair my falling house." It was now our "falling house," the earth, that needed repairing. The red heart of Scorpio pulsed and its tail was

DAVID AINLEY

Pigeon guillemot

poised, as if in warning.

A few petrels flitted about like swallows. The island below crawled with auk-lets, 100,000 strong, their croaking calls floating up to me on the light airs. When the auklets scurried through a window light, for they did not fly high enough to pass through the lighthouse beam, their gray eyes and white eye-brows flashed. Seeing a pair of eyes in the black loom of Lighthouse Hill, I got down on my hands and knees to investigate. Looking under a rock I saw a Farallon salamander, a species found nowhere but here. Its retinae shown orange-red, like reflectors; its brown body was stippled pale yellow. A form of arboreal salamander on an island without trees: this should give the nomencla-tors pause.

4-27 Partly cloudy. Wind ten to fifteen knots. White caps. We return to the mainland with the Coast Guard today. While waiting for the boat I began making a mental note of things that characterize the Farallones: the cormorants flying arrow-like to and fro; the wailing of the sea pigeons; the barnacle-clad backs of the gray whales; the rafts of California sea lions; the shining of the gulls in the light's beam; the skeleton of a pinniped in a sea cave; an octopus in Study Cave; a compact puffin in front of its crevice; elephant-seal bulls trum-peting; murres chattering and a tawny Steller sea lion gliding through the aqua-marine water of Sea Lion Cove.

The hoist was not working when Coast Guard search-and-rescue boat #41392 arrived at the island with a lighthouse service crew. Ron and Bob Fisher got the hoist going, and we departed on a quick trip to the mainland at 25 knots per hour. We glimpsed many loons and a few shearwaters as we plunged through the choppy seas, but it was hard to watch birds from this rearing, falling and yawing platform. Only Ainley could have done it – would have done it. We plowed through the Potato Patch and into the Golden Gate. A radio request had been received on the way to locate a dead whale reported beached near the bridge. We spotted a young gray whale on the sand near Kirby Cove, and it was duly reported. "Search-and-Rescue" dropped us at the Sausalito Yacht Club, and Bob and I walked to our car at the Clipper Yacht Harbor.

Frederick J Watson

VIII

Fledging of the Murres

From the pastures of the sea
from winter storm and wave,
to the Farallon Islands,
pilgrims of the flesh,
they come in droves
to breed in noisy colonies.

Under grey-blank skies,
on guano-covered spires
rising from boiling seas,
murres bow and bicker
and lay their pale egg,
on a bare ledge.

$\mathcal{S}$teve Morrell had long talked to me about the fledging of murres and promised to notify me of its advent this year. When he called, I was ready to go.

7-19-78 We departed from Yerba Buena Island at 0600 hours on a Coast Guard buoy tender. It was foggy, and the visibility was less than a mile. Only the unlit piers of the Golden Gate Bridge were visible; the span was completely obscured. Many of these days are dead calm, but there are some, and this was one of them, when there are big swells and wind gusts lurking in the fog. We proceeded down a vague corridor of blinking lights at Lime, Diablo and Bonita Points and Mile Rock.

A big feeding flock of brown pelicans and their attendants, Heermann's gulls, swarmed just outside the Gate. Murres, individually and in small groups, dotted the water. The ship, its wake smoke-filled, pitched and rolled in the swell. The smell of fuel and exhaust made me seasick. On big rolls the ship's bell rang, the clapper set swinging by the motion. The random sound of the bell played in my mind like a silly tune.

We saw many murres flying toward the Farallones with shiny anchovies in their beaks. It seemed odd they were feeding so far from the island. A few sooty shearwaters coursed stiffly over the swell. Nearer the island, we encountered the diminutive auklet diving for krill.

The island was truncated by fog, the base white-lined by breaking surf. When I had gotten in the car at four this morning, I had begun to smell guano; that aura gradually merged with reality as we came up to Southeast Farallon.

Steve Morrell, Craig Strong, a meteorologist and several volunteers were on the island. I had not been on the island with Craig since our trip with Dave six years earlier. A Coast Guard lighthouse maintenance crew and a biologist from the U.S. Fish and Wildlife Service landed with me. The biologist was given a brief tour and returned to the mainland on the buoy tender.

The gull chicks had not yet fledged, and the terrace was covered with these gangling creatures scurrying underfoot. The adults, as usual, dived and defecated on us. Morrell informed me it had been a poor year for cormorants. No pelagic chicks, and only a few Brandt's, had hatched. The double-cresteds had apparently fared a little better.

The murres were holding their own by flying long distances for anchovies, smelt and butterfish. Rockfish, their preferred food, was in short supply. The butterfish were too tall for the chicks to swallow easily, and other murres often stole them, which suggested butterfish was not ideal baby food and was only being used as an emergency source of nourishment. The crowded murre colony, which offers protection from gulls, also makes it hard for a parent returning with food to reach its chick without being robbed. Conditions of crowding, whether of humans in a city or birds on a ledge, are similar in their consequences. Though I am reluctant to admit it, the advantages for both must outweigh the disadvantages.

The food supply near the island was diminished because upwelling of cold water did not occur this spring, as reflected in the increased surface temperature of the water. If anything, warm water upwelled. The murres did better than the cormorants, because they were able to utilize distant food sources. Perhaps there were other reasons as well.

A pair of sea parrots fed a chick in a rock crevice near the murre blind. One adult returned with a line of fish debouching from its dilated beak. The puffin pursues a school of fish, turning first one way and catching a fish, then turning the opposite way and catching another. It lines the fish up, one facing left and the next right and so on. The fish are as neatly displayed in its beak as those in a market.

Below the blind the Brandt's cormorants, reduced in numbers, were in all stages of reproductive activity, from copulating to fledging. Most nests held one or two pale blue or brown eggs. In one nest three black newborn chicks, devoid of down, were writhing like snakes. In another, a single, large nestling waited to be fed. The lack of synchrony in nesting is atypical and the result of diminished food supply. The slightly lugubrious birds are usually the most interesting to watch, but today the murres were center stage.

The fledging of murres is one of the great dramas in nature. It is the greatest I have witnessed.

The stage was the murre loomery on Shubrick Point with cliff, surge channel and white water. A chorus of gull screams and murre gabble was backed by the symphonic boom and roar of the surf. The cast included gulls, murres, cormorants and oystercatchers. Seating was limited to the murre blind with a fresh breeze blowing in your face. Once the performance began, the only intermissions occured at night.

In 1978, biologists did not yet know which adult murre accompanied the chick in fledging. It was a natural bias to assume the mother played the central role. Later observations proved that it was the father. If you think of fledging in terms of an initiation, the father's involvement is logical. After leaving the cliff, the flightless chick and molting male wander at sea for six weeks looking for food. For the young bird, fledging is a hazardous undertaking: If it escapes gull predation and separation from the parent at fledging, it still faces starvation in the first few weeks of life.

For a method of observation, I used the single family history. I tried to pick out murres as early in the fledging process as possible and follow that family group until the murres were in the water and swimming away from the island; then I switched my attention to the next group. The volunteers in the blind with me were counting copulations, feeding encounters, etc., and they were unable to follow fledgings from start to finish. They were looking at populations, while I had the leisure of zooming in on a few individuals. The murre loomery is on a hill of variable steepness that leads down to the water. To the left is a high precipice overlooking a surge channel. To the right is the cormorant colony mentioned above. The murres either walk the long way down the hill to the surf's edge or proceed to the nearby cliff's edge high above the water. Western gulls, like centurions, are stationed around the colony and on the cliff face and patrol the skies above. Oystercatchers, bit players, poke among the rocks near the water for food.

When fledging begins, the chicks are one-third the size of the adult, not much bigger than the barnyard chicks sold from incubators. Their wings are poorly developed and, though helpful in balancing, are useless for flying and remain so for six weeks. The fledglings are dark above and white below, like the wintering adult.

An adult and chick leave the ledge – for this spartan species does not make a nest – and begin making their way through the crowded colony toward the sea. Sometimes both adults accompany the chick at this stage. The departure is preceded by a restlessness on the part of the youngster and an exercising of its wings. The chick appears to initiate fledging.

The progress is slow, as the chick must dodge the beaks of his own kind; it often stumbles and falls on the uneven terrain. As the small bird, awkward on land, climbs over rocks, falls off ledges and staggers downhill under the predatory gaze of the gulls, the tension mounts. If the longer route to the water's edge is chosen, the pair halt just beyond the reach of waves, and the adult flutters into the water and calls. The chick advances until it is swept off its feet and into the surf at its father's side. The chick then dives under the surf in a wonderful display of adaptability, and the two swim out to sea.

Fledging from the high cliff, 100 feet above the water, is more dramatic still. The cliff edge is closer and more easily obtained than the water's edge. Like the pinnipeds, murres are awkward on land and closer is better, perhaps even in the face of greater danger. Breeding murres return to the vicinity of their old nests the way salmon return to their natal stream, thus their fledging sites are also a matter of tradition.

The chick and its father arrive at the precipice after a short hike. There are three scripts from this point. In the first, the father, leaving the chick alone at the top, flies down to the water at the base of the cliff and calls. Soon the chick follows the example of its parent and leaps over the cliff. It flutters its ineffective wings to maintain balance, but inevitably begins tumbling end-over-end, bouncing off the cliff face, until it hits the water and swims away unharmed by its fall. Being light in weight has its advantages.

In the second script, the chick impetuously plunges over the precipice and tumbles down the cliff face and into the churning water before the adult, which immediately flutters down to its side to protect it from the gulls. What accounts for this difference in fledging behavior? Are there cues that the human audience does not perceive? What are the inner promptings? Do birds have personalities? Are some aggresive and others retiring?

In the third and least common of the variations of fledging behavior, the young murre approaches the jump-off point and then inexplicably turns back, the adult following without protest. The pairs I saw retreat stood by while other chicks fledged. The chicks did not fledge while I watched, for up to an hour in some cases. Was this a failure of nerve or of instinct? Or was it just stage fright? Perhaps the adult's entering the water first and calling from below is designed to prevent this behavior. Or maybe what the adult does is predicated by the position of the gulls.

The gulls watch for an unattended murre chick. They bolt the chick, much as a snake does its prey. They also rob one another: I had seen one gull take a fledgling murre from another gull at the foot of a murre cliff on Sugarloaf. I was told that gull predation of murre fledglings was much greater this year due to the shortage of seafood.

After four hours in the murre blind, I was stiff and cold. But I had witnessed a drama I was unlikely ever to see in the comfort of a theatre. The fledging is a marvel. (Though the word "marvel" is discredited from inappropriate and excessive use, the phenomenon is extant.)

On the way back to the house, I saw guillemots in their stylish plumage and bright red feet carrying little octopi to their young, a food source utilized only in lean years.

Common murres

Three boats lay off East Landing at anchor. One was a beautiful green motor-sailor *Bluenose*. The boats had come into the lee of the island for the night.

In the evening I went over to North Landing to watch rhinoceros auklets return to their burrows in a natural amphitheatre formed by Lighthouse Hill (Tower Peak) and Little Lighthouse Hill. In the past, you could walk over the saddle between the two Lighthouse Hills, but this way was now barred during nesting season to prevent disturbance of the rhinoceros auklets, puffins, guillemots and gulls.

Rhinocerous auklets are named for a small horn that develops at the base of the beak during breeding. These birds had a breeding hiatus here of 100 years, until 1974. Ainley and DeSante speculate that the introduction of rabbits, which occupied their burrows, led to their departure. The rabbits were recently eradicated from the island. In 1971 and '72, I frequently used to see these birds in the waters around Point Reyes. Now they were re-established on their traditional breeding grounds.

These dark-backed little birds with light bellies and rapid wing beats circled around the amphitheatre, their beaks crammed full of fish like a puffin, before alighting at their burrows and scrambling inside. Rhinoceros auklets are, as their ornamented beaks as well as their feeding habits suggest, more akin to puffins than to auklets. With the spotting scope, I could see adults resting outside in the vicinity of gulls. Their size protects them from the gulls, or else they are very bold. They have stout, pale-orange beaks and white nuptial plumes above and below the eye. Like guillemots, rhinoceros auklets enjoy sitting out "of an evening."

On the rocks at North Landing I saw a whimbrel or Hudsonian curlew. A willet cried out at my approach. A pair of nesting black oystercatchers lifted vermilion beaks and stared at me from vermilion-haloed, yellow eyes as they balanced on old-rose colored legs – as the birds are picturesquely described by Dawson in his *Birds of California*. Dave is partial to the black oystercatcher, which appears on the PRBO logo drafted by Helen Strong.

In the green water of Fisherman Bay, yearling sea lions porpoised and played.

Behind the boat house gull chicks, urchins with big legs and feet and small bodies, issued thin little cries for food. The voracious mother gull regurgitates food for her ungainly offspring, and then helps them eat it. The name gull is probably derived from gullet, which aptly describes the bird: a gullet with wings.

Adult gulls make a curious regurgitation display, which resembles feeding behavior except that nothing is discharged. The two make the display together a few times and then cross necks, as if making a pact. A little group of kibitzers gathers around to watch. Colonial nesters have no privacy, of course, but gulls seem to take more interest in the family affairs of their neighbors than do murres and cormorants, perhaps from hunger.

The fog settled slowly over the island until the peaks of Maintop, Sugarloaf and Tower were veiled. Then it imperceptibly dropped all the way down to ground level. The incessant cries of the gulls continued in the penumbra, punctuated by the thunder of big swells breaking in the surge channels and the low growls of Steller bulls.

7-20 Weather foggy. Wind northwest at 10 knots. It brightened a little by 11. At the cormorant blind, we watched guillemots flying in with food for their

Common murres

young. In describing the flight of the Auk family, Peterson in his *Field Guide to Western Birds* writes that they are "given to veering." This is especially true of sea pigeons. They dodge in and out, ruddering adroitly with their red feet.

And like the cormorants, they have fared badly this year. They fly as well as their relatives, the murres, but are unable to utilize the same food sources.

I recall Craig Strong, now a biology student following in Dave's footsteps, saying that it would be nice to have an oceanographer explain the causes for variations in the food supply. He bemoaned the fact that "all the pieces never get put together." Some of those pieces, such as the knowledge that changing weather patterns affecting local prevailing winds are a major factor in upwelling, have since been fitted together. The harvest of food by birds in the sea is little different from farming on land: it depends on weather and fertility.

The Farallones have the largest population of seabirds in the contiguous United States. A successful seabird rookery depends on offshore rocks or islands that are safe from land-based predators

Female California sea lion

and on the fertility of the surrounding sea, for there are deserts in the ocean as there are on the continent. The fertility of this section of coast results in part from the enormous outflow of fresh water through the Golden Gate. The Sacramento and San Joaquin Rivers and their tributaries collect snowmelt from the Sierra Nevada and Cascade Ranges and run-off from the foothills and Great Valley of California, meander through the Delta, pause in the Bay, and then pour a rich broth of fresh water and nutrients into the sea. The marriage of salt and fresh water produces abundant offspring of many kinds.

Pieces to Craig's puzzle are still being sought by researchers like Dave – and now Craig – through an interdisciplinary approach, one involving ornithologists, meteorologists, ichthyologists and oceanographers. Pollution, nets, overfishing and oil spills are other, newer pieces of the enlarging puzzle.

Craig showed me a northern fur seal at Sea Lion Cove. Hunted to extinction in this latitude, the species was now sending out representatives to old habitat in what is probably a reenactment of original patterns of distribution. The otariids – fur seals and sea lions – probably originated in the North Pacific. The fur seal is the most marine of the pinnipeds, spending six to eight months a year at sea. PRBO hopes it will someday resume breeding on the Farallones.

I went with Peter, a volunteer, to weigh Cassin's auklet chicks. Like storm-petrel chicks, they are balls of black down. Some were calm during the procedure and others struggled. The very young birds had a respiratory rate of 100 to 110 breaths per minute, and a heart rate of 180 to 200 beats per minute. The about-to-fledge birds breathed about 60 times per minute; the heart rate had declined to 120 to 140 beats per minute. During the period of most rapid growth, animals, including humans, and birds have correspondingly high metabolic rates reflected by fast respiration and heart beat.

At the murre blind, there was sporadic fledging activity. A chick was left on the cliff by the father, which flew down to a shelf below. A gull lunged for it, but missed as the chick leaped over the edge; the gull dropped quickly down on the chick and ate it before the father could intervene.

Another chick swam alone at the base of the cliff. After a while, it swam out a little way looking for the adult, then back toward the cliff. It then swam toward Shubrick Point, circled and returned, drawn back by the magnetism of the fledging point, where it was last united with the adult. Several adults were in the vicinity, but they paid no attention to the lost chick. I watched this drama within a drama for nearly 30 minutes. The orphan bobbed confusedly in the foamy swell like a bathtub toy. After drifting out, the chick again turned back toward the island. Suddenly a gull alit at its side and attempted to swallow it, but it somehow managed to escape. The chick then dove and came up six feet away. The gull lost interest. An adult murre then approached, calling, and the two swam around each other in a kind of dance. I thought the orphan was about to be reunited with its parent, when the two parted. The chick swam back to the base of the cliff, where I finally lost it among the cormorants riding the swell onto the island. I kept wondering what happened to this chick's father. Was it a young bird that abandoned its offspring? Was the chick lost, as a child is lost in a crowd when the parent is inattentive?

In the evening I went back to North Landing to watch rhinoceros auklets and puffins. I had to take a break once in a while from the intensity of the murre fledging. I saw a gull eating an adult Cassin's auklet. Many guillemots were loafing on the rocks.

The gulls keep up their din from dawn to dark. Whenever a gull reguritates food for its young, all its neighbors seem to step up their vocalizations. Twenty-five thousand Western gulls inhabit the Farallones – about one-half the total population, all of which occurs along the West Coast from Canada to Mexico. The gull is a very successful species and has many affinities with man. The garbage of the latter is the proverbial free meal of the former. Both are noise polluters. Many of both species are ill-mannered, and they are both great opportunists. Whatever happens to other species, I think these two will keep each other company until the end. (I heard that the western gull was John Smail's favorite bird. Perhaps he admired its hardihood as a species, in which it resembles *Homo sapiens*, with whom it was his job to deal as director.)

7-21 A willet dived at us as if it were protecting a nest, but it does not breed here. Perhaps it was pretending.

At Sea Lion Cove, there were several Steller bulls with large open wounds on their massive necks from earlier territorial disputes. A large pup was nipping at its mother to make her roll over so it could suck. Young bulls were sporting in the water with females. One female ran quite a distance over a rocky shelf to escape the attentions of a bull. Their grace and speed in the water appears to give them great delight, which is perhaps heightened by their labored progress over the sharp rocks where they haul out – rocks that were described by one visitor as being "very hard on shoe leather."

I went with Steve to weigh and band guillemot chicks. We pulled them from marked crannies in the rocks of Lighthouse Hill. The guillemot nest cavity is bare. The chicks still had a remnant of the egg tooth on the upper mandible. Unlike mammals, birds must break out of the fetal microcosm.

In the afternoon the seas were calm, so Steve, Peter and I put in the Boston whaler for a tour around the island. A large sea-elephant bull had been seen on West End, and Steve wanted a look at it. I wanted to take pictures of Great Arch Rock. Steve went down in the boat, and Peter and I followed in the Billy Pugh. Just off East Landing, a pod of California sea lions was swimming by; Steve cut the motor and we drifted to watch them. They porpoised through the water with such effortlessness and verve that we were all half-mesmerized. We gradually became aware of a long shadow in the water passing lazily around the little boat. The water was clear, and when our attention was redirected toward this new phenomenon, we could see that it was a shark passing a few feet below the surface. It circled again, rising closer to the surface, and passed alongside the boat. It was longer than the eleven-foot whaler. The perpetual grimace, probing eye and pulsing gills were too close for comfort. The girth at the pectoral fin was quite large, and the slender tail undulated in an almost leisurely fashion. It was silver-gray above and white below. We were all impressed with this close-up view of a great white shark, but rather than study it further, we quickly started the motor and sped off toward Murre Cave. Now we understood why the sea lions were swimming with such alacrity. We joked nervously and kept a weather eye out for dorsal fins, as we drifted off Shubrick Point to watch for murres returning to the island with food for their young.

We found two dead murre chicks floating in the water. I wondered if they had gotten separated from the adult like the one I watched yesterday and had been wantonly killed by gulls. On other occasions, I had seen gulls kill murre chicks and leave them uneaten. The explanation that gulls were taking more murre chicks this season to supplement their diet seemed inadequate to account for their killing, without eating, chicks. Like man, they seem to kill for the pleasure of it.

Many adult birds – rhinoceros auklets, murres and guillemots – swam near the island. Pelicans, like gargoyles, adorned the rough-hewn crest of Great Arch Rock. We also saw many of them on Sugarloaf and the beaches of West End. Off Indian Head we saw two chick-parent pairs of murres – the only ones we saw. We tried to make out the Indian's head on the rocky prominence of that name.

We got back in time for me to visit the murre blind before dark. The odyssey of the murre chick from its rocky ledge to the surf breaking around the island reminded me of Tom Thumb's ordeal. The murre chick's warble, when it rejoins its parent in the water after fledging, if translated into human language, would probably echo Tom's answer when asked by his father where he had been: "Down a mouse hole, in a cow's stomach, and in a wolf's maw and now I shall stay with you." The murre chick would answer that it had been on a high cliff, in a heavy surf, and in a gull's bill!

When I arrived, I saw a few fledging pairs standing at the edge of a low cliff

DAVID AINLEY

Common murre

above a rocky terrace leading down to the water. Fog had begun to veil the island. I saw several successful chick-parent pairs in the surge channel, but the cliff above was hidden in fog. As it grew darker, more and more fledging pairs began to desert the colony and move down toward the sea.

Many of the nest sites were on a cliff above the terrace. The chicks had to get off the cliff without the benefit of a cushion of water below. These mercifully waited until it was almost dark, when the exodus was at its peak and the gulls much less dangerous. The chicks plunged off these ledges – some as high as 30 feet – with reckless abandon. Slightly stunned, their fall unbroken by the impotent beating of the immature wings, they rested before resuming their march to the sea. Under cover of fog and approaching darkness, they streamed down – now more commonly in groups of three. Whether both parents or one parent and a "neighbor" accompanied the chick was difficult to ascertain. If they began as a pair, the third murre might join them at the jumping-off point, flying or walking up from the water. Sometimes, if three began the trek, one would leave the group half-way down and fly into the water. Soon after, it would swim up in the surf and come ashore, walking toward and calling the adult and chick. It might accompany them for a ways and then, as if by example, return to the water, call and wait. Once I saw the third murre walk past the fledging pair and very deliberately place itself between them and nearby gulls! Tuck, in his work *The Murres*, thinks that the third murre is not the other parent, but a nonbreeder. The advantage of two adults participating is apparent: The chick is never left unattended – and I expect survival is greatly enhanced. Then the question inevitably arises: Why aren't two adults always involved? No shortage of unengaged murres exists. And while we're asking questions, we might as well ask why all murres don't wait until twilight or fog to fledge? Why do pairs attempt fledging in broad daylight, when their chance of success is least? If the chick, prompted by a surge of sex and adrenal hormones, does initiate fledging, then the process is chemically controlled and questions of when and where are probably irrelevant.

I watched until it grew dark. In the gloam I could see above the black surface of rock only the two heads, tilted inquisitively and quietly waiting, silhouetted against the white water that ringed the island. Then two shadows, one large and one small, leaped into the sea. This scene kept repeating itself, until I could no longer see anything.

I climbed down from the blind, giddy with the experience.

7-22 I arose early. It was foggy and calm. I ate quickly and went over to the murre blind.

The colony was abuzz with the rasping, motor-like calls of the adult murres, interspersed with the strange, musical warbles of the chicks. The young sounded like songbirds, the adults like rusty ratchets. I spotted several incubated eggs, one a lovely powder-blue dripped with chocolate brown. Another was buff-color with similar dark drippings. I saw several abandoned eggs not yet raided by the gulls. Dave told me later that eggs laid this late in the season were infertile. They were now rotten, and even the gulls would not eat them. I found it hard to believe there was something proteinaceous that gulls wouldn't eat!

There were no murres fledging at this early hour. So many fledged yesterday that I half-expected it all to be over. Many adults, probably females whose chicks had fledged or died, were returning to the colony with fish. One such adult landed below the blind with a torn fish. After being harrassed by its neighbors, it flew away, only to return a short while later still with its torn fish.

Another murre landed with a fish. It was undisturbed by its fellows and stood for 30 minutes with the fish in its beak. Now and then the murre would place the fish beneath its breast as if it were feeding a chick. The chick had probably fledged with the father while its mother was on a protracted food search far from the island.

A spirited fight took place, the first I had seen between murres. Beginning as a routine squabble with the usual bill-fencing and grating call, it erupted into a full-scale battle. One bird was repeatedly driven off, but would not give up. It kept returning and sidling up to the dominant bird to renew hostilities. The white breasts of both birds were soiled with dirt. The loser dripped blood from its beak. The fight was finally finished when the victor clamped its beak across the other's neck, almost suffocating it. Struggling free, the vanquished murre stood where it had been driven, its wings hanging partially open, its mouth agape and panting.

Though the hour was late, the urge was present: some mating was still occurring. The foreplay superficially resembled quarrelling: fencing with the beak and the gutteral racket. Then the male hopped nimbly on the female's back, flew in place and tucked its wagging tail under the female's. Afterwards, the female walked forward letting the male drop off. Perhaps these were young birds or birds that had lost an egg or chick. This late union would not result in a chick.

Returning from lunch, I saw that the first fledging pairs had begun to congregrate near the precipice. They were waiting calmly, not yet ready to descend. Whatever draws them into the sea had not yet begun to exercise its full power.

Just before noon, the drama began. Two pairs advanced toward the edge of the cliff above the surge channel. A gull, sentry-like, manned its post at the foot of the cliff. One pair moved to a new vantage point away from the gull, and the chick fledged safely. The parent of the other chick fluttered off the precipice and landed on a ledge partway down the cliff – the only instance of this I saw. The chick bravely took the plunge and tumbled to a stop almost at the gull's feet. The gull lifted its wings to fly over and devour the helpless chick when the parent flew down between them, saving the day. Regaining its composure, the chick leaped into the water, and the parent quickly followed. If safety is in numbers and the single purpose of life, survival, how do you explain singular and *ipso facto* dangerous behavior? Mere aberration? If the life history of the bold fledgings could be known, might some survival value for the species result from their presence? Might they pioneer a new colony or discover alternate and possibly distant food sources in a lean year, such as this? Might these birds be more resistant to disease and hunger? Once the study of individuals begins, as it already has for gulls and Brandt's cormorants on Southeast Farallon, we may eventually get answers to these questions. The opposite is true of man; population studies will explain his future. Robinson Jeffers, in his poem "Rearmament," puts it best:

> The beauty
> of modern
> Man is not in the persons but in the
> Disastrous rhythm, the heavy and mobile masses, the
> dance of the
> Dream-led masses down the mountain.

Six or seven successful fledging attempts from the high cliff took place this afternoon. Only one chick fell victim to the gulls; it was left on the rocks uneaten.

Close parental supervision protects a chick; parental carelessness dooms it most of the time. An expression of community-oriented behavior among murres is the involvement of non-breeders in fledging. These subadults are probably preparing for the season when they will have fledging chicks of their own.

A parent-chick pair on a ledge below the blind began the long trek to the water's edge. The chick luckily climbed down from the ledge to the ground below, because a leap in daylight, when few others were fledging, would likely have been fatal. After the laborious descent from the ledge, the pair began making its way through the cormorant colony and a small cluster of murres residing on the more gently sloping aspect of Shubrick. The chick appeared programmed to climb up onto every rock as a vantage point from which to gage its progress toward the sea. Then it tumbled off again. The pair reached a low ledge above the intertidal rocks, which were exposed by the low tide. They climbed down past the gulls and headed to the sea over rocks cobbled with mussels and festooned with seaweed. A shelf of rock for which the pair headed jutted out over the breaking waves. The longest fledging journey I had witnessed was about to close successfully, when for some inexplicable reason, the parent fluttered into the water five feet from the brink. The chick began to struggle forward after its parent, when a gull descended on it and grasped it in its beak. Two oystercatchers feeding nearby witnessed the assault and began diving and screaming at the gull, in what appeared to be a deliberate attempt to free the murre chick. They drove the gull hither and thither, but it would not relinquish the chick. In spite of the oystercatchers' interspecific attempt at aid, the gull killed the chick and left it. Several other gulls inspected it, shook and poked it, but did not eat it. I found myself irrationally angry at the adult murre for its seemingly impetuous behavior.

A train of fledging murres departed between 2:00 and 3:00 P.M. In all my observations today, only one parent accompanied each chick. I began following one pair just as they approached the brink. At that point, a single chick joined them, its parent foolishly already having flown into the water, as occurred in the last instance. The remaining parent let its chick fledge alone into the swirling surf and took the other in tow. The lost chick then fledged, and I think all the relationships got sorted out in the water.

Shortly thereafter, another single chick presented itself on the verge. An adult murre emerged from the water and claimed it before the gulls did. More chicks were getting separated from parents as the rush to fledge increased and confusion set in. Eventually, their antiphonal calling would reunite most of them.

The chicks fledge on an incoming wave and are often carried back by the wave's advance, before being drawn into the sea by its retreat. They can easily be stranded; if the wave is a big one, it may be awhile before another of similar size will carry them out. To have struggled down to the sea and then to be pushed back and stranded by the very element which, but a moment before promised salvation, is a cruel, Dickensian fate. One chick caught its foot in a crevice and, struggling and beating its downy wings, seemed certain to fall prey to the gulls. Yet, after two or three waves failed to free it, a big swell rescued it and carried it to the side of its calling parent.

Like human fathers with their sons in tow, adult murres and chicks moved toward the open sea through the rings of foam that encircled the island.

From the door of the murre blind, I saw the boat that would return me to the mainland tied up to the buoy at East Landing. I made a quick descent; greeted Harriet Huber, who was coming on the island; jumped on the Billy Pugh; and descended into the waiting whaler. We motored out to the sailboat

Lara skippered by Fred Walker. On board was Fred's father, a retired professor of biology and cytology from a small Mississippi college. I had hardly expected the company of a fellow southerner in such a place, far enough from the South to enjoy the flavor of its accent without the shadow of its bigotry. We chatted amiably on the way in.

As it was calm, we motored. I saw a number of adult and fledgling murre pairs swimming away from the island. Gradually the enchanted isles, *Los Farallones de los Frayles*, were swallowed up in the fog. Landmark and beacon to the mariner, larder to the pirate, Russian and San Franciscan, and furrier to the world, the Farallones have played an important role in the history of the West. As natural laboratory, herald of environmental health and wildlife haven, let us hope they have an equally significant part in the next century.

We ran through the Golden Gate close to the north shore to avoid the strong rip of the outgoing tide and suddenly emerged from the windy, turbulent strait with its gloomy fog and sodden cold into the brilliant sunshine of San Francisco Bay. Fog overflowed Wolfback Ridge; Angel Island and Belvedere were bright in the late afternoon sunshine; Sausalito was huddled in shadow; and rising above the fog Mount Tamalpais was serene and aloof. As the sun dropped behind the fog bank, the breeze freshened and fine little ripples ran across the darkening water.

THE END

Adult murre and chick departing Southeast Farallon

MURRE

Uria aalge

for Dave Ainley and Steve Morrell

I.

From the pastures of the sea
from winter storm and wave,
to the Farallon Islands,
pilgrims of the flesh,
they come in droves
to breed in noisy colonies.

II.

Penguins of the north,
they return faithfully
year after year,
old and young,
to the same precipice,
making their obeisance.

III.

Under gray-blank skies
on guano-covered spires
rising from boiling seas,
murres bow and bicker
and lay their pale egg,
on a bare ledge.

IV.

One of the sea tribes,
with chocolate cape
elegantly creased

behind eye of black onyx,
ochre mouth color
revealing its ardor:

V.

The egg, pale blue
dripped with brown,
is brooded between
wrist and breast.
Hatched, the chick stands
bravely against the winds.

VI.

Before the chick can fly,
when it barely walks,
the trudge to the sea
begins with wing-beating,
then climbing down
under the gull's frown.

VII.

The adult and chick descend
through the milling crowd,
peer into the surge
from the edge
where they stand
as if hand-in-hand.

VIII.

A hundred feet below
the surf booms
in the narrow channel
and hisses out,
the way down cordoned
by gulls like centurions.

IX.

The father flutters down,
the chick following,
tumbling through the air,
bouncing off the cliff face
into the sea
diving quickly.

X.

If it is grounded
or can't reach the father
in the chaotic surf,
a gull swallows it
in a scene so obdurate
Nature herself cries out.

XI.

Far from the island
on the ocean plain
in search of fish,
flightless,
chick and father
wander together.

XII.

The murre loomery
is now vacant
and wrapped in fog.
The sea-girt island
is silent of bird:
Only wind and wave are heard.

Notes

1. Francis Drake's name was given to the bay where he careened and repaired his ship *Golden Hinde*. Although the bight under the lee of Point Reyes Headland, which was the original San Francisco Bay, has been called Drake's Bay in recent times, the use of the possessive of Drake is anomalous and unnecessary. In this text I will follow the historian H. H. Bancroft and use the designation "Drake Bay" for the aforementioned body of water.

2. A report issued by California Department of Fish and Game in 1980 documented more shark attacks on humans at Tomales Point than elsewhere on the California coast. The shark attack rate between Año Nuevo and Bodega Bay is 10 times greater than it is for the rest of the coast. (Calif. Fish and Game, 67(2): 76-104 1980)

3. *Trentepohlia aurea*. Richard Plant told me it was an algae and not a lichen, as I supposed, and Al Molina of College of Marin identified it.

Books Useful to the Author

Allan, Grover M. *Birds and Their Attributes*

Choate, Ernest A. *The Dictionary of American Bird Names Revised Edition*

DeSante, David F. and Ainley, David G. *The Avifauna of the South Farallon Islands, California*

Ennion, Eric. *The House on the Shore*

Jeffers, Robinson. *Collected Poems*

McMinn, Sean. "Migration Stations" *Birdwatch Magazine* January 1992

Nelson, Brian. *Seabirds*

Point Reyes Bird Observatory Newsletters

Point Reyes Bird Observatory Farallon Log

Ray, Milton S. *The Farallones, The Painted World and Other Poems of California*

Scammon, Charles M. *The Marine Mammals of the Northwestern Coast of North America*

Scheffer, Victor. *Seals Sea Lions and Walruses*

Speich, Steven and Manuwal, David A. "Gular Pouch Development and Population Structure of Cassin's Auklet" *The Auk* April 1974

Steinbeck, John. *Logbook from the Sea of Cortez*

Terres, John K. *The Audubon Society Encyclopedia of North American Birds*

Tuck, Leslie. *The Murres*

United States Coast Pilot 7 Pacific Coast

Viola, Herman J. *Exploring the West*

COLOPHON

Published in an edition of 1400 paperback and 100 hardback copies by La Ventana Press in 1998. Design and production by Elizabeth Morales of Point Reyes Station, California. Printed and paperbacks bound by McNaughton & Gunn, Inc., of Ann Arbor, Michigan. Typeface for the text is Goudy and Goudy Small Caps.

ABOUT THE AUTHOR

Michael Whitt has practiced medicine in Point Reyes Station, California for the past 25 years. He and his wife Barbara have two children, Garrett and Lazuli. He is a life member of Point Reyes Bird Observatory.

ABOUT THE ARTIST

Frederick J. Watson is a well-known wildlife painter in Europe. He owns and operates the Kittiwake Gallery at the National Nature Reserve of St. Abbs Head on the coast of Southeast Scotland. He exhibits in both Britain and the U.S. and has been a frequent visitor to California since 1980. Derick has been one of the artists invited to show their work at events organized by the Royal Society for the Protection of Birds and has exhibited with the Society of Wild Life Artists since 1989. He presents the annual Kittiwake Gallery Award for unestablished artists, whose work shows promise and evidence of in-depth field studies. In 1994 and 1997, Derick's watercolors were selected by the Leigh Yawkey Woodson Art Museum in Wausau, Wisconsin for its annual "Birds in Art" exhibition. He has also illustrated a regional bird book, *The Birds of the Sheffield Area* (in Britain), and written and illustrated articles for wildlife and conservation magazines.